# FIGHTING STRATEGIES OF
# MUAY THAI

*Fighting Strategies* of *Muay Thai* is dedicated to all those who teach and practice the fabulous art of Muay Thai, especially to the good and generous people of Thailand.

# FIGHTING STRATEGIES OF
# MUAY THAI

## Secrets of Thailand's Boxing Camps

## Mark Van Schuyver

### with Kru Pedro Solana Villalobos

Paladin Press • Boulder, Colorado

*Fighting Strategies of Muay Thai: Secrets of Thailand's Boxing Camps*
by Mark Van Schuyver and Kru Pedro Solana Villalobos

Copyright © 2002 by Mark Van Schuyver and Kru Pedro Solana Villalobos

ISBN 1-58160-358-4
Printed in the United States of America

Published by Paladin Press, a division of
Paladin Enterprises, Inc.
Gunbarrel Tech Center
7077 Winchester Circle
Boulder, Colorado 80301 USA
+1.303.443.7250

Direct inquiries and/or orders to the above address.

Visit our Web site at www.paladin-press.com

# TABLE OF CONTENTS

The Counter Fighter
The Elusive Fighter
The Tricky Fighter
Overview of the Universal Fighter

# FOREWORD BY AJARN SIRA MESAMAN

have known Kru (instructor) Pedro Villalobos as friend and student for many years. I am very happy to report that *Fighting Strategies* of *Muay Thai* is among the best books on Muay Thai ever written and is certainly the most comprehensive book of Thai fighting strategies ever to be published. Martial artists around the world will benefit from this work.

Thanks from all of us at the Buddhai Swan Institute in Thailand to Kru Villalobos for sharing his extensive knowledge of the art and thanks to Mark Van Schuyver for formulating this excellent book.

—Ajarn Sira Mesaman

*(Ajarn Sira Mesaman is the international head trainer of Buddhai Swan Sword Fighting and Old Muay Thai Institute in Thailand.)*

# FOREWORD BY TONY MOORE

met Pedro Villalobos in Thailand at the Buddhai Swan School in Bangkok. Mae Kru Mesaman invited Pedro and me to lunch with the Mesaman family. He did this to formally introduce us as brothers in the martial arts of Thailand and the fellowship of Buddhai Swan. During the meal Pedro and I talked about our many and varied experiences in Thailand. Pedro told me that his goal was to visit, and hopefully train at, 100 camps in Thailand. He spoke of researching and compiling information on the art and bringing it back to the West.

I felt an immediate connection to Pedro, and he and I have remained friends since our first meeting at Ayuddhaya. Pedro has returned to Thailand many times to continue his quest to learn all that he can about Muay Thai. To date, he has trained in at least 46 different Thai camps. He is a fighter and also a scholar of both Muay Thai and *krabi-krabong*. The depth of Pedro's commitment to Muay Thai and his knowledge of the art are staggering. I am deeply honored to recommend this excellent book that contains the best of his research. *Fighting Strategies of Muay Thai* will put you on the pathway to discovering the beautiful art of Muay Thai.

—Tony Moore

*(Tony Moore is chairman of the British Muay Thai Boxing Council, president of the European Muay Thai Union, the former vice-president of the International Federation of Muay Thai Associations, the British Light Middleweight Champion of 1993, a judge and referee of more than 1,000 Muay Thai bouts, a student of Por Kru Samai Mesaman of the Buddhai Swan Institute, and a ninth-degree gold sash in krabi-krabong.)*

# ACKNOWLEDGMENTS

I would like to thank Kru Pedro Solana Villalobos, owner, director, and head instructor of the Thailand Arts Institute, for sharing without reservation his immense knowledge of Muay Thai boxing. I am also grateful to Thailand Arts Institute instructor and fighter Richard "Tchalla" Trammell for sharing his perspective on the art, as well as to all of the students, instructors, and fighters at Villalobos' Thailand Arts Institute.

Additionally, I am deeply grateful to the people of Thailand for generously sharing their national art with the world. I offer very special thanks to those Muay Thai instructors in Thailand who have opened their camps and their hearts to students from around the globe.

Finally, I express my gratitude to my parents, J.C. and Billye Van Schuyver; my fiancée, Dessa; and my children, Holly, William, and Sarah, for their encouragement of and support for this important project.

# PREFACE

hen the Western martial arts community discovered Muay Thai boxing in the latter half of the 20th century it got a very big surprise. Again and again the slightly built Muay Thai boxers dominated all challengers from China, Japan, the United States, and other countries. In contest after contest the Thai boxers used their devastating knee, elbow, fist, foot, and shin kicks to put down all those who dared to enter the ring with them.

The Western press covered the story of Muay Thai's superiority in detail. Thai boxers were routinely featured on the front cover of the major Western martial arts magazines. Within a very short period every serious martial artist in the world who had a concern for open competition was aware of the Muay Thai boxing phenomenon. Practitioners of countless styles were forced to benchmark themselves against the proven power of Muay Thai. Almost overnight, Muay Thai revolutionized the world standard for martial arts effectiveness.

After these demonstrations of superiority, Muay Thai techniques quickly found their way into many other styles. Western kickboxing, for example, was very strongly influenced by Muay Thai in a remarkably short period. Today, many no-holds-barred fighters and virtually all the mixed-martial-arts specialists include Muay Thai techniques in their systems. For instance, shidokan karate's mixed-martial-art matches feature marathon contests in which fighters must go three rounds of bare knuckles, three rounds of Muay Thai boxing, and three rounds of submission grappling. Thus, Muay Thai has infiltrated the thinking and the practice of the martial arts around the globe.

As Muay Thai became known in the West, the early trend was for established martial arts schools to include Muay Thai techniques in their existing systems. This trend continues, and more and more traditional Muay Thai schools are found in the West. These traditional schools generally teach the same techniques as the nontraditional variety, but their method and manner for training are different.

The main difference between a traditional and a nontraditional Muay Thai school is that the traditional schools also teach the cultural and traditional aspects of the art. One will see, for example, fighters from a traditional school wearing the *mongkon* headband, sealing the ring before the match, and most importantly, performing the *wai kru* ritual (respect for the teacher) and the *ram muay* (boxing dance) before fighting. Traditional fighters always demonstrate respect for the ring, their teacher, and the art in this highly stylized manner, while nontraditional fighters may not.

Pedro Solana Villalobos' Thailand Arts Institute in Atlanta, Georgia, is one such traditional school. Villalobos and his trainers teach all aspects of Muay Thai fighting while simultaneously adhering to the traditions and cultural norms practiced in Thailand.

Villalobos believes that respecting the culture is important and following the code of behavior set down by the ancient Muay Thai masters is key to maintaining the purity of the art. In his view, following and respecting the ancient traditions are what maintain Muay Thai's integrity as a timeless martial art and prevent it from becoming just another ring sport.

## ABOUT KRU VILLALOBOS

Kru Pedro Solana Villalobos is one of the most knowledgeable and experienced Muay Thai fighters and instructors on the East Coast today. He began his fighting career in his native country of Spain and lived in several Western countries before finally settling in Atlanta. He is the owner, director, and head instructor of the Thailand Arts Institute in Atlanta.

As of this writing, Villalobos has more than 15 years of experience in the martial arts. He began his studies of the martial arts at the age of 6 with the art of judo and then later migrated to kickboxing and Thai boxing. Despite his success in the ring, Villalobos knew that something was missing in his fight game. After many years of

Pedro Solana Villalobos (second from left in "Shark" shorts) with some of his training associates at the Ososhapa gym in Bangkok, Thailand.

Villalobos in the So Vorapin gym in Bangkok, one of the more than 45 Muay Thai training camps he has visited in Thailand.

training he felt that his progress was at an impasse. Villalobos realized that getting to the next level, that of a world-class Muay Thai fighter, would mean actually training in Thailand and studying Muay Thai from practicing masters of the art. To fulfill his dream, Villalobos packed his bag and bought a ticket for Bangkok to seek Muay Thai training at the source. He did this because he was frustrated with the many variations and mutations of Thai boxing that he had encountered in the United States and in Europe.

Although many of Thailand's Muay Thai training camps are in Bangkok, the capital and largest city, there are camps scattered throughout the country. Examples are the Sidyontong gym in in Pattaya, the Sakuapan gym in Kanchananburi, and the Paton gym in Ayuttaya.

When Pedro arrived in Bangkok in December 1998, he had no idea where or how to look for Muay Thai training. He spoke no Thai and had no local friends or contacts to guide him. He made his way through the bustling crowds, being careful not to bump into anyone. He carried a black duffel bag filled with Thai shorts, bag gloves, hand wraps, and a few necessities. Finally after many hours of searching in the heat he found a Thai camp. He politely requested permission to train. The trainer spoke to him briefly and then promptly turned him away.

Villalobos was undaunted by this initial rejection. His heart full of passion for the art of Muay Thai, he pressed forward in blind faith. Eventually he found a Thai camp that opened its doors to him. Pedro stayed at the camp for some time. He trained hard, behaved respectfully, and quickly proved that he was indeed a serious Muay Thai student.

The trainers soon realized that Villalobos had good intentions. They saw that his heart was that of a real fighter and that his head was in the right place. In other words, they judged him worthy of their time.

After this short proving period, Villalobos was literally overwhelmed with Thai hospitality. Sensing his trustworthiness, his new Thai friends introduced him to a larger circle of Muay Thai contacts. Over the next 13 months, Pedro was welcomed to and trained at as many as 45 different Thai boxing camps. He also studied krabi-krabong, Thailand's ancient martial art for warriors that features both weapon and empty-hand fighting and Thai massage. He was treated like a family member almost everywhere he went.

When Villalobos returned to his adopted home in Atlanta, he was forever changed as a martial artist. The walls of his Thailand Arts Institute are now covered with pictures of him with students and trainers from the camps that he visited on his first Thailand trip, as well as photos from his annual return visits.

Villalobos observed a number of variations in style as he crossed the Thai countryside. The differences, however, did not alter the spirit of the art or the connection felt among all Thai boxers across Thailand and, indeed, around the world. Muay Thai creates a powerful, some say spiritual connection, between fighters. This is due in part to the sacred traditions of Muay Thai and the bonding that takes place when fighters live, train, and fight together in a brotherhood.

When Villalobos returned to the United States, his confusion and frustration were totally gone. No longer does he question how and why Thai boxing should be taught or fought. He knows how and why. The totally authentic routines and methods that Villalobos practices and teaches his fighters are explained in detail in this book.

Today Villalobos has rank in several styles. He is a professional fighter and trainer. In other words he is a full-time martial artist.

Villalobos is certified in the following areas:

- Second-degree black belt kickboxing (FEKB) under Mariano Anton, president of the Spanish Kickboxing Association
- Instructor of Muay Thai, Thai Boxing Association (TBA, USA), under Ajarn Suruchai Sirisute
- Black belt instructor (Wing Chun Association of the United States) under Sifu Francis Fong
- Eighth-degree gold sash instructor (Wat Buddhai Swan Sword Fighting Institute, Thailand) under Mae Kru Mesaman
- Instructor of Muay Thai (Wat Buddhai Swan Institute, Thailand) under Ajarn Mae Krub Mesaman
- Instructor in massage (the Wat Pho's, Thailand) in foot massage, traditional Thai massage, and therapeutic acupressure massage
- Blue belt, Brazilian jiu-jitsu (Gracie Association) under Royce Gracie

Villalobos is the southeastern United States representative for the Wat Buddhai Swan Temple of Thailand, the foremost authority on krabi-krabong, and the official trainer of the Thai royal family and military.

Kru Villalobos is also a successful and experienced fighter: he has fought in many matches in several different countries. His many accomplishments as first an amateur and now a professional fighter include the following:

- 1994 Light Middleweight Kickboxing Amateur Champion of Spain (World Association of Kickboxing Organizations [WAKO])
- The U.S 1998 International Sport Kickboxing

Association (ISKA) Middleweight Muay Thai Champion in the professional division

- 1998 champion of Submission Open in Griffin, Georgia
- 1998 SFO lightweight champion
- 1998 ISKA (USA) middleweight Muay Thai champion
- 1999 Battle of Koh Samui (Thailand) champion

Villalobos is more than just a professional Muay Thai fighter and instructor. He is a serious scholar of the Muay Thai way. He goes to Thailand for several weeks each year to research and learn the art in all its aspects. He respectfully passes his vast knowledge of Muay Thai and krabi-krabong to his students with joy and without reservation.

Kru Villalobos can be reached by email at <thailandartsinstitute@hotmail.com>.

# 1

# MUAY THAI BOXING

any people believe that Muay Thai is the most effective stand-up martial art system that the world has ever produced. It is the national sport of Thailand and has become a popular sport worldwide. Muay Thai is, however, more than a fighting system and more than just a ring sport; it is an ancient method for transforming oneself into the best person possible. Muay Thai is a time-proven method of self-discovery and personal development in which beating an opponent is not nearly as important as the physical, mental, and spiritual growth that take place during the process of training and practicing. Participation in the art of Muay Thai is a cultural experience in which one journeys with the intention of developing the self, serving other, and serving the world.

This book covers every aspect of Muay Thai, including strategies for victory in the ring never published before. Experienced Muay Thai fighters and new students alike will benefit enormously from the exploration of Muay Thai that follows. Practitioners of every martial art will find the proven techniques, strategies, and tactics explained in this book to be invaluable.

First consider that there are many books on the techniques used in the martial arts. Techniques are important to be sure, and the fundamental Muay Thai techniques are covered in this book. These, however, are simply not enough to guarantee victory in the Muay Thai ring—or on the street. Tactics are also required, and even more important, combat strategy must be employed.

People are often confused about the definitions of *strategy* and *tactics,* but most everyone knows what is meant by *technique.* Technique simply means this or that physical activity done this or that way. Punches, elbow strikes, kicks, knee strikes, parries, and footwork are just a few of the techniques of Muay Thai.

Tactics and strategy are often misunderstood. Understanding the true definition of tactics and strategy is important to understanding the wisdom shared in this book. Both of these concepts are derived from ancient Greek. The following definition describes both of these critical terms perfectly.

> To the Greeks, *taktikos* meant "fit for arranging or maneuvering," and it referred to the art of moving forces in battle. *Strategos* was the word for "general." Originally, therefore, strategy was the "art of the general," or the art of setting up forces before the battle. In military terms these definitions still apply; with them in mind, you can easily see why strategy must precede tactics in a military setting. Before you can fight at Gettysburg, you've got to get to Pennsylvania (S.E. Heiman, D. Sanchez, and T. Tuleja, 1998).

You can see that strategy is the business of preparing to fight and tactics refers to the way you move and what you do during the fight. Strategy is what a fighter plans to do before the blows begin. Without strategy the best techniques are virtually worthless. And without tactics techniques are extremely limited. All three elements are important, but strategy it is the real key to victory in any form of combat.

Just as it does in war, strategy must come before tactics in Muay Thai and in all types of competitive, self-defense, and survival-focused martial arts. Techniques, therefore, are most valuable when intelligent strategy and excellent tactics are employed before and during the fight. A complete explanation of the fundamental techniques and principles of Thai boxing and a thorough overview of Muay Thai boxing strategies and tactics are in this book, with the primary emphasis on the strategy of employing tactics and executing techniques to achieve victory in Muay Thai fighting.

## A BRIEF HISTORY OF MUAY THAI

Where did Muay Thai techniques, strategy, and tactics come from? The history of Muay Thai is rich and ancient. It is a story of evolution both physical and spiritual. To fully understand Muay Thai, you must delve deeply into its history. Perhaps the best place to begin is with a brief examination of one of the parent arts, known today as krabi-krabong.

### Krabi-Krabong

Muay Thai, as the world knows it today, is the descendant of an ancient Thai martial art for weapons and barehanded fighting known by several names, including krabi-krabong. The armies of ancient Siam (now Thailand) taught krabi-krabong and its empty-hand pugilistic component to all of its citizen soldiers.

The krabi-krabong techniques were continually advanced, developed, and perfected through the reality of deadly combat. The way of Muay Thai spread through the civilian population, and over time it became a significant part of the culture.

Krabi-krabong is still practiced today. A few Westerners, including Villalobos, have been certified to teach this ancient art. Students at Villalobos' Thailand Arts Institute learn the art of krabi-krabong, including its empty-hand system sometimes called Muay Thai Boran (old Muay Thai).

### Muay Thai Boran

Muay Thai Boran is a generic term for any of the Muay Thai systems that existed in Thailand before the art became regulated by the state in the early part of the 20th century. According to Villalobos, Muay Thai Boran is the forerunner of modern Muay Thai. Krabi-krabong's system of empty-hand fighting is, therefore, an old Muay Thai Boran. The version of Muay Thai Boran practiced at the Thailand Arts Institute is literally a component of krabi-krabong. It is not possible to classify Villalobos' style of Muay Thai Boran as something separate from krabi-krabong.

The history of the old Muay Thai is sketchy because krabi-krabong dates back many centuries and evolved through the turmoil of many wars and political changes and through the hands of many war masters. Muay Thai Boran emerged at a time when history was mostly passed down orally. The few writings that survive provide validation of the oral histories, including the historical account that dates back at least eight centuries.

Villalobos says krabi-krabong's empty-hand systems (Muay Thai Boran) employs the natural weapons of the human body in imitation of the ancient weapons of war. For example, the arms are used like swords, the shins are conditioned to strike like a staff, the elbow and knee are used like a war ax, the fist operates like the tip of a spear, the foot works like an arrow or pike, and the head hits like a war hammer.

In ancient days, if a soldier lost his weapons on the battlefield, he would fight on using his natural body weapons. Meanwhile, civilians practiced Muay Thai Boran boxing, adopting it as both a martial art and a community sport. Gradually krabi-krabong's empty-hand boxing became part of the fabric of Thai culture.

It is written that in the 12th century A.D., in the period known as Sukhothai, Muay Thai Boran prizefighting was already a favorite pastime of the Siamese people. By then every village had its local Muay Thai champion. Fortunes were won and lost wagering on Muay Thai Boran bouts. Oral history relates that young men of all walks of life sought out the Muay Thai Boran masters in hopes of training, fighting, and gaining fame and recognition. Muay Thai Boran camps, the legends say, sprang up in villages all across the land.

This tradition of personal boxing competition continued for hundreds of years all through the Sukhothai, Ayutthaya, and Rattanakosin periods leading up to the early part of the 20th century. During these centuries Muay Thai fighters typically fought with bare knuckles. Sometimes they wrapped their hands in rope, mostly to protect the knuckles. On occasion the hand wraps were dipped in sand or glass to add danger, blood, and excitement to a match.

Head butts, groin strikes, and eye gouges were completely legal in the old days, as were many other dangerous and excessively damaging techniques. Countless destructive and even lethal techniques were employed in the Muay Thai Boran contests fought through the centuries.

Modern Muay Thai has been described as somewhat brutal by Western observers. In truth, modern Muay Thai is downright civilized in contrast to the ancient Muay Thai way. The Muay Thai Boran battles were truly no-holds-barred

events in which fighters were commonly maimed or killed. Muay Thai Boran was more than just brutal: it was lethal.

Much of the wisdom of the Muay Thai Boran experience survives today. Lessons learned in combat by the ancient fighters and trainers have been passed from generation to generation. Kru are still teaching the ancient Muay Thai Boran combat and no-holds-barred competition skills at krabi-krabong schools in Thailand today. A handful of non-Thai instructors, such as Villalobos, are teaching the old ways in the West.

**New Muay Thai**

In the 1920s and 1930s Thailand officials began to regulate Muay Thai competitions. Slowly Muay Thai Boran became the "new" Muay Thai, or Muay Thai boxing as it is known today. Over some time the rules became formalized and ring conditions were standardized.

Thai boxers were ultimately required to wear gloves and groin guards. Head butts, eye gouges, groin strikes, and other excessively dangerous techniques were restricted and finally eliminated from the sport. Muay Thai stadiums were built to display the new sport. The new state-regulated Muay Thai sport flourished for several years.

World War II restricted Muay Thai's resurgence. Soon after the war, however, the new Muay Thai bounced back with renewed popularity. Bangkok quickly and firmly established itself as Thailand's hub of modern Muay Thai competition.

Today Muay Thai matches happen daily and are witnessed live by hundreds of fans. Fights broadcast from such major stadiums as Rajdamnern and Lumpinee are among the most popular of all televised programs in Thailand. Muay Thai has finally become known to the outside world and is gaining in popularity as an international sport.

**Muay Thai International**

Muay Thai fans are springing up in many parts of the world including the Americas, Holland, Finland, Russia, and Japan. Muay Thai is being advanced worldwide by such governing bodies as the World Muaythai Council (WMC) at <http://www.wmtc.nu/>.

At least two amateur international Muay Thai boxing associations exist today. One is the

International Amateur Muay Thai Federation (IAMTF) <http://www.iamtf.org/>. The IAMTF organized the first world amateur Muay Thai championships in 1995. Another amateur sanctioning group called the International Federation of Muay Thai Amateur (IFMA) <http://www.wmc-ifma.com/>, IFMA gained fame when it conducted the Muay Thai competition known as "World Cup 2000."

International Muay Thai amateur rules require fighters to wear head gear and protective vests. In the United States, state laws sometimes regulate amateur and professional bouts. In some cases use of the elbow is restricted or eliminated from competition.

In other events pads must be worn on the elbows, but headgear is not allowed. From the various restrictions applied by different states, it can be safely said that the United States has simply not made its mind up about Thai boxing.

Meanwhile Muay Thai continues to gain international popularity. A general understanding that Muay Thai can be safely practiced is emerging. For instance, it been accepted as an official sport in the Asian Games competition, and there is a concerted effort to have Muay Thai added to the list of Olympic sports.

There is no doubt that Muay Thai boxing has great appeal to the martial arts community in general. Each year, the number of people practicing Muay Thai grows significantly as more schools open worldwide. All over the world, martial artists are seeking instruction in authentic Muay Thai technique. Some train to increase their overall skills as marital artists; others train to become Muay Thai fighters. An informal interview conducted by the author with dozens of mixed-style marital artists revealed that Muay Thai is considered by a significant majority to be the best stand-up fighting style in the world.

Some traditional Muay Thai schools are now open in the West in addition to the many mixed-martial-arts schools and others that teach Muay Thai technique. One such traditional school is Villalobos' Thailand Arts Institute.

## OVERVIEW OF MUAY THAI STRATEGIES

It is important to understand that the history and proper practice of Muay Thai has many interpretations. Different masters use a variety of approaches to training, strategy, and technique. There are many excellent methodologies for training, and it would be impossible to cover them all. The methods taught in this book are totally authentic and have proven themselves effective in the ring.

Ultimately every fighter develops his own style, and no two fighters perform in exactly the same way. It is the responsibility of every Muay Thai student to find his own way of fighting. My goal is to share one proven method and explain it in great detail while simultaneously expressing respect for the many other proven methods that exist in Thailand and across the world.

The Muay Thai techniques, strategies, and tactics in this book are those taught by Kru Pedro Solana Villalobos. It is not my nor Villalobos' intent to diminish or overrule training methods and systems used by other instructors. The Muay Thai art is simply too complex and diverse to pigeonhole or make any such judgments about "right and wrong" approaches to training.

Now it is time to peer deeply into the world and workings of Thai boxing. This commences in the next chapter with an evaluation of Muay Thai's upper-body offensive and defensive techniques.

# UPPER-BODY OFFENSIVE AND DEFENSIVE TECHNIQUES

uay Thai upper-body weapons include fists and elbows, and a relatively small variety of punches and elbow strikes make up the full upper-body arsenal. In some situations fighters are allowed to use the shoulder. Head butting is no longer permitted in official Muay Thai matches.

There are six basic Muay Thai punches: (1) jab, (2) cross, (3) front-hand hook, (4) back-hand hook, (5) front-hand uppercut, and (6) back-hand uppercut. However, many variations of the six basic punches exist. The techniques are simple and extremely versatile. To the observer Muay Thai punches look a lot like Western boxing punches. There are, however, some important differences.

Thai fighters must defend against more than just punches, so their defensive positions and responses are different from those of Western boxers. For example, Muay Thai fighters typically hold their hands higher and at a wider angle than Western boxers. In the Muay Thai basic guard position both of the fighter's hands are at eyebrow level. Some fighters allow the thumb of their right hand to rest just above the ridge of their right eye. The left hand is at the same height, usually 3 or 4 inches in front of the face. The elbows are away from the body. There should be a distance of approximately one fist between elbow and torso. This position offers maximum protection from incoming fists, elbows, and feet. In the guard position the hands and knuckles face the target and the chin stays down. The body is completely straight so that when a fighter throws any body weapon he can recover very quickly.

It is important to know that the position of the hands changes as the fighter moves from farther to closer range. In Muay Thai there are four ranges: kicking, punching, elbow and knee, and clinching. At the

Full stance.

Fighting stance.

kicking range, the fighter opens his hands more. At boxing range, the hands close in some to cover the face more. At elbow and knee range, the hands pull in very tight to the face and body. At this range there is no space between elbows and body. In clinch range, the guard position goes away and both fighters grab the neck when space appears between the bodies.

The strong leg is back and the other leg is slightly forward in the Muay Thai guard position. The torso faces the opponent, and the hands form a frame from the level of the eyebrows down and out. The angle of the arms resembles a steep roof. Holding the arms in the guard position is also important for achieving maximum power, speed, and recovery for every Thai punch.

Thai boxers fight with wrapped hands and boxing gloves. When they punch, they attempt to land the blow evenly across all their knuckles. No effort is made to isolate the contact point to specific knuckles. In every Thai punch, the wrist is bent inward slightly.

Muay Thai fighters draw the power for their punches from the earth. Power is channeled through the hip and shoulder almost simultaneously. Punches do not return to the guard position along a straight line. Jabs, crosses, and hooks all end with a downward motion. The punching hand returns to the guard position in a circular fashion after delivering its power. The position of the elbow is stable during the entire punch to maintain positional control.

Under the rules common to most Muay Thai associations, fighters can use their fists, elbows, shoulders, knees, shins, and feet to attack or defend. Head butts are not allowed in modern Thai boxing, but in the old days they were common and perfectly legal.

It is easier to identify the very few illegal targets in Muay Thai than the reverse. Fighters are not allowed to strike the groin deliberately because it can be a temporary showstopper. Fighters are not permitted to strike the back of the neck because it can be a permanent showstopper, possibly resulting in death.

It is legal to kick the back, hips, coccyx, and kidney area. Fighters are discouraged from deliberately spiking the spine. Most Thai referees, however, consider hits to the spine to be the fault of the one who gets hit and do not take these fouls especially seriously. Such a violation might only result in the loss of a point during a match. That's about it. In general fighters can hit anywhere else, even to the knees.

Sweeping is also allowed, but there are strict limits. Fighters can hook the neck and throw. It is legal to grab a limb and kick the supporting leg out from under an opponent. It is not legal to throw an opponent over one's hips or to sweep his ankle. Fighters cannot shoot into an opponent and grab one or both legs low to throw in the style of wrestlers and submission grapplers. For the most part, Thai throwing techniques rely on redirecting the energy of the opponent. Thus Muay Thai throws more closely resemble some of the techniques seen in aikido than those most common to wrestling, judo, and jujutsu. It takes tremendous skill to throw with these limitations especially since the fighters are wearing gloves.

## SEVEN POWERS OF MUAY THAI

There are seven forces that must be aligned in most Muay Thai strikes: (1) transition, (2) velocity, (3) rotation, (4) snap, (5) torque, (6) triangulation (or reverse triangulation), and (7) gravitation. If coordinated properly, these seven types of energy harmonize to create an amazing blast of power. To illustrate, consider the following example of how a fighter might throw a punch at an opponent using his rear hand.

The action begins with a transition from one spot to another. Transition is a horizontal movement of the entire body. A forward, backward, or sideward motion of the body can create transition. Thai fighters employ forward transition when they move in toward an opponent to close the gap and at the same time deliver a punch or kick.

Jack Dempsey was speaking of the same concept in his classic book *Championship Fighting, Explosive Punching, and Aggressive Defense* when he wrote, "You can launch your body-weight into fast motion, and, like dynamite, you can explode that hurtling weight against an opponent with a stunning, blasting effect. . . ." (Dempsey, 1950, 7).

### Transition

Transition helps to generate momentum. Webster's definition of momentum is "the quantity of motion of a moving object equal to the product of its mass and its velocity." To understand momentum, imagine that a person is in outer space wearing a space suit and standing with his feet strapped to the International Space Station. In his hands he holds two balls: a baseball and a big, dense metal ball. On Earth the metal ball weighs 100 pounds. In space, however, both balls have zero weight. Imagine that 20 feet away is another person standing on the station, feet strapped in place, preparing to catch the balls. The first person throws the weightless baseball. The second person catches it easily in one gloved hand.

Now the first person holds the dense metal ball in his hands preparing to throw it. Remember that on Earth it weighs 100 pounds. The person throws the weightless metal ball. The second person lifts both hands to catch it but is knocked onto his back. Why would the dense metal ball have this effect and the baseball not? Because the momentum of the heavier ball exists in space just as it would on Earth. Each object has mass, and the metal ball has a lot more than the baseball. When thrown, the speed and mass of the dense bowling ball create momentum that is much greater than that of the baseball, even in the weightlessness of outer space. The experience of catching it in space would be similar to catching it on Earth.

### Velocity

The second power derives from velocity. Webster defines velocity as the "rate of change in position in relation to time." Mass plus velocity equals momentum. In this space station example, both the mass and the speed of the object thrown amplify the amount of energy received by the person who catches the weightless ball. Transition without velocity has minimal momentum. Velocity without the mass of the body delivers minimal momentum. Thus the first two energies—transition and velocity—combine to create and amplify momentum.

### Rotation

The third energy is called rotation power, and it comes from the hip. According to Webster, to rotate is "to turn around or cause to turn around a center point or axis; revolve." Now picture the fighter in this example moving quickly with forward transition toward the target. The fighter rotates his hips and upper body, adding more energy as he drives the punch forward. This counterclockwise rotation of hips and torso, when done fast and in synchronization with the forward transition, adds significant power to the right-handed strike.

### Snap

The fourth power is called snap, and it is added as the fighter snaps his shoulder as he rotates his hips. For all upper-body strikes snapping power comes from the shoulder. Snapping power is also derived from the foot for roundhouse kicks. Webster describes snap this way, "to break, part, or be released suddenly, esp. with a sharp, cracking sound." This snapping motion adds a whip-like velocity to the already speeding punch. Consider that at this moment in the example transition power, velocity, rotation power, and snapping power from the shoulder are already fueling the punch.

### Torque

The fifth possible energy is called torque. Webster defines it this way, "a twisting or wrenching effect or moment, exerted by a force acting at a distance on a body, equal to the force multiplied by the perpendicular distance between the line of action of the force and the center of rotation at which it is exerted." Torque occurs as the fighter turns his wrist, spinning it overhand into a horizontal position and driving the knuckles into the target.

At this point in the example the fighter's fist is at the apex of its potential. The fist is now being propelled and powered by five energies. The full momentum of the punch is landing on the target. In effect, energy from the ground is passing from the fighter's feet to his hips and into his shoulder and then through his arm and fist in a fluid, unified action. At this moment in the example, using five of the seven energies, this punch is already very powerful and may do a lot of damage.

Consider, however, what might occur to the energy of the punch from the point of contact if a fighter uses only the five powers described so far. If the fighter pushes straight into the target, the momentum will carry forward or possibly bounce back. If the power goes forward, especially if the fighter should miss the target, he is in danger of going with it. So much momentum may carry the fighter's body forward and might even cause the fighter to lose his balance. If the fighter hits the target and it yields, there may still be a moment of forward-transition imbalance. If the target is very hard, then the energy will rebound, shocking and perhaps jarring the fighter's arm. To avoid these limitations, the Thai fighter drives the striking fist downward at this point, thus adding the sixth energy, triangulation.

### Triangulation

To understand triangulation it is necessary to go back to the beginning of the action in the example. The fighter prepares to punch and brings energy from the floor, propelling himself in forward transition. His speed amplifies the power. Simultaneously, as his forward foot lands, he rotates his hip, bringing the energy and momentum up his back. The fighter adds power by snapping the shoulder and turning the fist to add torque power just before impact. Rather than allowing the energy to travel forward in a straight line, the fighter adds the sixth power of triangulation by pushing his fist downward upon impact. The fighter literally drives the energy into the target and down toward the ground.

The Thai fighter's fist rides this downward circle like a wave and returns like a whip to the guard position. Thus the energy is "triangulated" from the fighter's feet, up through the body and shoulder, out through the arm and fist, into the opponent, and then back down to the ground under the opponent's feet, where it theoretically rebounds.

The closest word in English to explain triangulation is "drop." Webster defines drop as a "sudden fall, descent, slump, or decrease." Triangulation is more than just dropping the punch. It is a physical and a mental effort to direct the energy downward into the target and retrieve it through the earth. Triangulation may also be thought of as a form of leverage. Point A is at the fighter's feet. Point B is the place at which the fighter's fist contacts the opponent. Point C is the ground beneath the opponent's feet.

Here is another example of pure triangulation, and in this picture one can easily see the leverage points. Consider a jujutsu or no-holds-barred fighter who straddles his opponent in the mount. In this dominant position he is basically riding on the other fighter's torso, pinning and holding him tight with his thighs. Imagine that a punch is delivered on the man below and that the fist strikes the prone man's face. The energy of the punch passes through man's head, and his skull thumps the floor of the ring. Thus energy is triangulated from the mounted fighter's grounded, locked, and seated position through his arm downward into the opponent's face and then into the ground. The effect is horrific. The referee typically stops most no-holds-barred fights after just a few such skull-crushing triangulated blows.

It is a bit harder to triangulate a punch from a standing position than from the ground in a mounted position. The power and control that triangulation gives the stand-up fighter is so significant, however, that it must not be overlooked or underdeveloped by the serious student of Muay Thai. Triangulation is one of the many high-level talents that Thai fighters cultivate and one of the skills that sets them apart from many other systems.

### Gravitation

The seventh energy that must be harmonized in Muay Thai fighting is gravitation. Webster defines this power as "the force by which every mass or particle of matter, including photons, attracts and is attracted by every other mass or particle of matter." Of course, the power of gravitation has been at work in all of the examples above. No conscious effort has yet been made to understand its effect and use it to

the fighter's advantage. Gravitation and its effects on the fighter are discussed in detail in an upcoming section.

The seven powers—transition, velocity, rotation, snap, torque, triangulation, and gravitation—appear to some degree in most of Muay Thai offensive techniques. For easy reference, a chart describing each of the powers follows.

### DESCRIPTION OF POWERS

| | |
|---|---|
| Transition | Energy gained from motion relative to the opponent's position (e.g., stepping toward the opponent) |
| Velocity | Speed of the body and of the body weapon as it approaches the target |
| Rotation | Turning of the hip when delivering a strike (e.g., turning the hip to add power to a punch) |
| Snap | Quick forward motion of the shoulder done when punching or throwing an elbow (also refers to the sharp turning of the foot when delivering a Muay Thai kick) |
| Torque | Spinning of the hand during a punch just before impact (this energy occurs only in punching) |
| Triangulation | Dropping of the hand, elbow, or foot upon impact with the target that drives the energy of the strike downward (e.g., downward force at the termination of a punch) |
| Gravitation | Pull of the Earth (the critical power that makes all Muay Thai techniques possible) |

The basic techniques of Muay Thai and their source of power as derived from the seven possible energies described above are covered in detail below. In all the fighting examples that follow assume that the fighter is right-handed.

### JAB

The Muay Thai jab is delivered with the lead hand. For a right-handed fighter this is the left hand. A few fighters have really powerful jabs capable of causing serious damage to an opponent's face. Most fighters use it as a setup for the delivery of more serious power from a cross, an elbow, a knee, or a

The jab with the front left hand.

Defending the jab with the back hand.

kick. Jabs are very fast and are without doubt a vital part of the Thai boxer's tool kit.

If a fighter is right-handed he creates the guard position with the left foot and left hand leading slightly. The left hand is held high at 3 to 4 inches in front of the face with the thumb at eyebrow level. The left elbow is away from the body at a distance of about 3 inches.

To fire off a jab from a gap-closing forward transition motion is common. Velocity is critical. Because a Thai fighter keeps his torso facing the opponent, the second energy of rotation occurs as the hip and torso turn clockwise. Since the lead hand is already forward, the degree of rotation is slight. In this, as in most punches, the Thai fighter snaps the shoulder upon delivering the punch. The left hand spins horizontally near the end of its flight, adding torque to the strike.

Impact upon the target occurs across all knuckles of the left hand. At the point of impact the Thai fighter presses downward, forcing the energy from the punch to triangulate to the earth below the opponent's feet and thus amplifying power and allowing for the quick and circular return of the left hand to the guard position just above the eyebrow. The jab is performed with very little motion of the elbow to maintain control and to protect the centerline and the left side of the head and upper torso.

Thai fighters release air and make noise when they throw a jab or any strike. They say letting sound out with the punch or kick releases energy that keeps the body from getting overly tired. The sounds vary from fighter to fighter. Typical sounds are *taa, rum, ohh, geeep,* and so on. Villalobos recalls that every Thai fighter that he observed in his travels to Thai camps made noises like this when they punched.

It is also important to blow the air out of the lungs during a strike for defensive reasons. When the air is expelled from the lungs, the abdominal muscles tighten. If a fighter is counterpunched in the body with air in the lungs, the effect of the blow is much more harmful. Air in the lungs creates a space, and when a blow lands it compresses and shocks the organs, sometimes to the point of causing knockout. Fighters should therefore blow out air when delivering the jab and all other Thai strikes, including punches, knees, elbows, and kicks.

## CROSS

The Muay Thai cross is a very powerful punch. It is delivered with the strong hand from the guard position. A right-handed fighter's left foot is forward so the right hand has a greater distance to travel to the target. The right cross takes more time, but it generates much more power than a left-handed jab.

Full view of right cross.

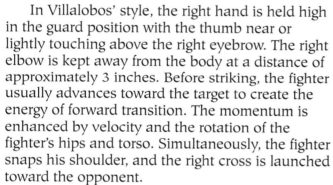

Defending against the cross with the front hand.

In Villalobos' style, the right hand is held high in the guard position with the thumb near or lightly touching above the right eyebrow. The right elbow is kept away from the body at a distance of approximately 3 inches. Before striking, the fighter usually advances toward the target to create the energy of forward transition. The momentum is enhanced by velocity and the rotation of the fighter's hips and torso. Simultaneously, the fighter snaps his shoulder, and the right cross is launched toward the opponent.

The wrist of the fighter's right hand curves downward slightly to ensure that the impact occurs evenly across the top knuckles. Just before impact the fist turns to the horizontal, adding the power of torque to the blow. Immediately upon hitting the target the fighter's fist drives downward, pressing the energy of the blow into the floor below the opponent's feet and generating triangulation energy.

The right hand rides the triangulation energy wave back in a circular motion. The punching hand does not snap back; rather, it circles back. The return motion is whip-like and is performed with the elbow in place to control the center. The punch is complete when the right hand returns to the guard position. The seven powers are clearly evident in the Thai cross.

## FRONT HOOK

The front hook is used to reach around the opponent's guard. It can be done during an advancing or a retreating motion, and the power it delivers is significant. A right-handed fighter will likely deliver the front hook with his left hand. The weapon can be applied against head or body targets.

Like all the Thai punches the front hook originates from the guard position. The left hand is held a few inches in front of the face with the thumb at the height of the eyebrow. The hand lowers when the fighter moves forward or backward, gains velocity, and rotates his hips. The shoulder snaps, and the punch is launched on a horizontal plane. The fist turns to a position horizontal with the floor, and the wrist curves downward slightly. Contact is made with all the knuckles of the left hand. Upon impact, the fighter drives his fist downward to triangulate and then allows the hand to whip back to the guard position in a circular fashion.

The seven powers are also at work in the front hook. The fighter creates transition energy by advancing or retreating, adds power with velocity, rotates the body clockwise to create rotation energy, snaps the shoulder to create snap energy, rotates the fist to create torque, and then drives the fist downward upon impact to create triangulation

Front left hook, variation one.

Front left hook, variation two.

power. This punch, like all the others, is performed with a complete, unified body action, never an isolated arm motion. A hook thrown with the arm alone would be virtually useless.

When fighters throw a front hook, they pivot the front foot inward so that the toes of either foot point toward each other during the rotation phase. A hook thrown with the body using the seven energies is hard to see coming. The front hook is surprisingly powerful and can be very damaging.

## REAR HOOK

Should the reader at this point have doubts about the need for all seven energies in the striking process, he is encouraged to glove up and experiment with a partner. Have the partner hold a Thai pad or focus mitt and try each punch using or not using some or all the motion energies. The increase in power with the addition of each layer of energy can be felt.

For another view of the energies in action and to add to the reader's overall understanding of the energies, including the importance and power of gravitation in Muay Thai fighting, consider the rear hook. First think of the hook as it would be done here on Earth and then imagine how it might look if you tried it in space.

When the rear hook is performed here on

Earth, transition energy is created as the fighter moves forward. Speed is added. He rotates the hips and torso counterclockwise to create rotation power. At this time the rear foot pivots so that the toes of either foot point toward each other. Next the fighter snaps the right shoulder for a velocity boost, turns the wrist in the horizontal plane for torque, arches the hand around the opponent's guard, and presses the fist downward to create triangulation energy as it strikes the target across all knuckles. The fist returns to its guard position following a circular path. The result of this punch done with six powers in the pull of gravitation is devastating.

Now consider the same fighter facing an opponent in the near-zero gravity of high Earth orbit. Imagine both fighters gloved up and once again standing inside the International Space Station. In this example their feet are not strapped down. Suddenly one fighter pushes his foot against the floor in an attempt to close the gap. Rather than move forward toward the opponent, however, the attacking fighter rises up slightly because the vector of his forward motion is not governed by gravity. The fighter gathers only part of the expected momentum from transition energy and velocity as he approaches the target.

As he nears the opponent, imagine that the attacking fighter rotates his hips and torso, snaps his shoulder, turns his wrist in the horizontal

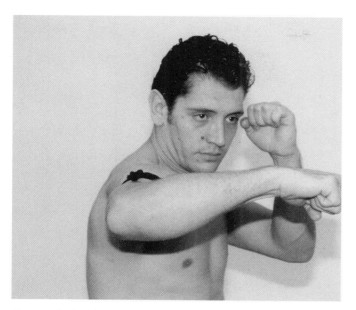

Rear right hook, variation one.

Rear right hook, variation two.

plane, and smacks the other space fighter across the jaw. Not much of the transition power or the rotation power makes it into the fist because the fighter's feet are no longer on the floor and his body is not anchored by gravity.

As his fist lands, the attacker presses his fist "downward" in an effort to triangulate the blow. Only a tiny amount of triangulation power results. Without the power of gravitation, pushing "downward" with the punch into the opponent's body results in sending the attacker bouncing slightly "upward" and the opponent slightly "downward."

If measured, this right hook in space would likely have very little power. The six controllable powers of movement have been dissociated, uprooted, and severely limited or eliminated by the lack of the seventh source of energy, gravitation.

Understanding the role of gravitation in Thai boxing helps us realize that most of a fighter's power comes from his connection to the earth. Thus you can see that gravitation provides leverage for attack and defense. Gravitation is the essential energy source for virtually all strikes. Although it is true that you cannot control gravity, it is absolutely critical to include it in all calculations for the execution of Muay Thai techniques. It is important to align with gravity, which is another way of saying that balance is also critical.

## FRONT AND REAR UPPERCUT

The uppercut is a sneaky punch that can be done with either the left or right hand. As always, the fighter works from the guard position with the hands near the eyebrows and the elbows an inch or so away from the body. The front-hand uppercut is quicker and less powerful than the rear-hand version. Both are considered short-range punches.

Occasionally a fighter will use the front-hand uppercut to initiate an attack. This is rare because most fighters prefer to use the jab to begin an exchange.

The rear-hand uppercut is typically used in a combination. The chin is the primary target for both uppercuts. Uppercuts come from an angle outside the opponent's guard and then move to the center. The punching hand returns to its position near the eyebrow in a straight line.

Muay Thai uppercuts differ somewhat from boxing and kickboxing uppercuts. Typically, Muay Thai fighters do not bob and weave lest they receive a knee to the face for their troubles. Lowering the hands is also unwise. Unlike boxers, Thai fighters launch the uppercut with virtually no dip of the punching hand.

For the uppercut, the arm extends forward and drives upward into the opponent's chin. The typical angle of the strike is about 45 degrees. It

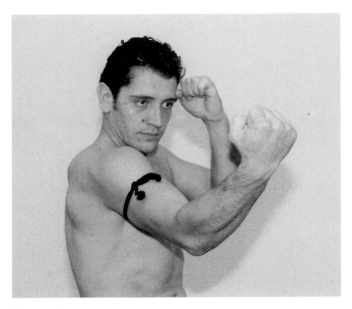

Rear right uppercut.

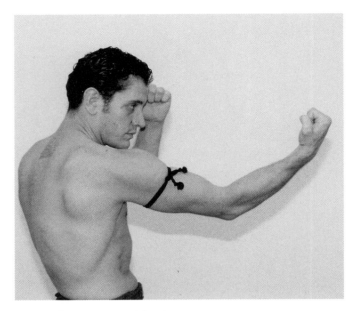

Rear right uppercut, side view.

is hard not to telegraph any type of punch, and the rear uppercut, unless used deceptively, is especially easy to see coming. Dropping the hand tends to give this punch away, as well as exposing the head to attack. Lowering the hand gives the punch additional power, but the risk is too great for a Muay Thai fighter to take.

The uppercut is powered by transition, velocity, rotation of the hip, snap of the shoulder, torque of the wrist, and of course gravitation. Since the energy is delivered upward, this punch does not triangulate downward to the earth. Instead it uses reverse triangulation to complete the circle and keep the momentum from traveling too far forward. Reverse triangulation is acquired by curving the rising punch, thus driving power up from the ground into the target and yet retrieving some of it, in theory, by the circular follow-through of the hand as it returns to the guard position.

Jabs and lead-hand uppercuts are frequently used to test the opponent and set up for combinations. Done in isolation the front-hand uppercut is fairly hard to see coming, but it has less range than the jab. In general, uppercuts require the fighter to be in very close proximity. This is especially true for back-hand uppercuts.

Thai fighters in Thailand use a special L-shaped wall bag to practice uppercuts. Heavy bags do not work well because Thai uppercuts travel at upward angles. The uppercut is not

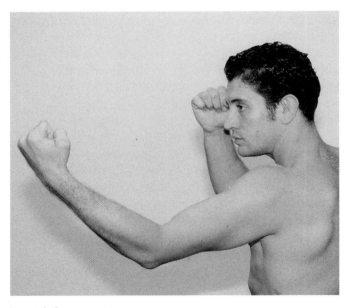

Front left uppercut.

common technique for Thai boxers. Some Thai fighters are good at it, but the jab, cross, and hook are favored by most.

## ELBOW TECHNIQUES

For Muay Thai fighters, the elbow is an essential weapon. These are the three basic elbow techniques of Muay Thai: (1) horizontal, (2)

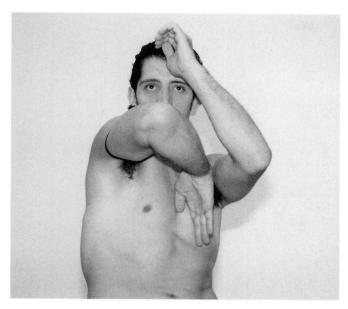

Right horizontal elbow ready to be employed and in use.

Right horizontal elbow against Thai pad.

downward, and (3) upward. There are variations on the three basics that have to do with adjustments in the angles of attack. There are at least six specialty elbows used in Muay Thai boxing: the spinning back elbow, climbing elbow, flying elbow, invisible elbow, spearing elbow, and ear strike elbow.

Elbow strikes are powerful and damaging. Unlike the hands, elbows are not padded during Muay Thai bouts in Thailand. There is no muscle covering the tip of the elbow, so the likelihood of its causing a cut is very high. Muay Thai fighters hit with the intent of slicing their opponents with the outer tip of their elbow rather than clobbering them with the forearm.

Despite their power, well-placed elbow strikes do not usually result in a full knockout. Countless technical knockouts, however, are created when elbow strikes open gashes to the head, which sometimes require 10 or more stitches to repair. The elbow is extremely effective at close range and in the clinch or when done in combination with kicking and punching techniques.

The elbow is considered a short-range weapon. It is extremely uncommon for a fighter to engage an opponent using an elbow as a first strike. Typically kicks, punches, and knee strikes are used to close the gap and create an opening for the elbow. Muay Thai boxers are experts at using the elbow in the clinch.

## Horizontal Elbows

The horizontal elbow is the most basic elbow strike and one of the more powerful elbow strikes. Imagine a situation in which a fighter has managed to get into very close range with an opponent. The opponent lowers his left hand, and the fighter, seeing the opening, advances slightly and fires a right horizontal elbow to the face. Energy for this strike comes from the ground, and power is added from velocity and momentum gained as the body moves in. Rotation of the hips and snap of the shoulder send the elbow in a horizontal path to the target. The tip of the elbow strikes the opponent's face with tremendous speed and power.

At the moment of contact, the fighter drives the tip of his elbow downward to create triangulation energy and to initiate a circular motion that allows the quick and relatively safe return of the arm to the guard position.

Fighters can launch the horizontal elbow, and all the basic elbows, from the guard position. They may also launch elbow strikes following any punch and without returning to their guard. In the case of a right horizontal elbow, the right hand is held at the right eyebrow very nearly to the point of impact. After impact the right hand returns to the right eyebrow, and the elbow circles back to recompose the guard position. Thus the

Basic left horizontal elbow.

Villalobos grabs the neck of his opponent to fend off a left horizontal elbow and attacks with his own left elbow.

fighter exposes himself for only a tiny fraction of the time taken to throw the technique.

Mechanically the horizontal elbow is similar to the Thai hook. The same powers are in play, including transition, velocity, rotation, snap, triangulation, and gravitation. Only torque power is missing. Left and right horizontal elbows operate in the same way, with the left elbow being quicker because it is closer to the opponent and the right elbow having more power because the hip has more rotation space. The most common target for the horizontal elbow is the face. The chin and eye are especially desirable strike points because of the high probability of causing a cut and scoring a technical knockout.

### Downward Elbows

Downward elbows happen at various degrees. They might, for example, come straight down or down at a 45-degree angle. The body mechanics of the downward elbow are almost identical to those of the right cross. For a downward-elbow strike the body moves forward with speed to gain momentum. Simultaneously the hips rotate, the shoulder snaps, and then the elbow flies forward, with the arm turning slightly and gathering a small amount of torque. Upon the impact of the strike, the fighter drives the elbow downward to ensure triangulation. Gravitation makes it all possible.

Villalobos defends himself against a left horizontal elbow with a right upper elbow.

The right hand stays near the right eyebrow during the strike. It sticks like glue to this protective position as long as possible. Just before impact the hand is lifted and then returned immediately to the defensive spot above the right eyebrow. The elbow returns to its guard position in a circular path after impact.

Left downward elbow.

## Upward Elbows

Upward-force elbows differ from horizontal and downward elbows because they reverse-triangulate upon impact. The upward elbow is structurally the same as the uppercut. This strike is done only in the very closest of proximity to the opponent. It is executed inside the opponent's guard.

The upward elbow is often used in clinch situations. In most circumstances the upward elbow is aimed at the chin; it can return safely and quickly to defensive position. As with the other elbow attacks, the hand of the attacking arm is kept near the eyebrow for as long as possible. The arm returns to its guard position as quickly as possible. Exposure to counterattack is minimal. In the case of the upward-elbow strike, there is virtually no time at which the hand leaves its defensive perch near the eyebrow.

Some Muay Thai fighters are elbow

Villalobos delivers a right downward elbow to the top of his opponent's head.

Right upper elbow.

Left uppercut elbow.

specialists. Their basic strategy is to get in close and work with elbows and knees. These close-range specialists tend to be shorter fighters; taller competitors often favor the longer ranges. Strategy is a very personal thing, and there are many exceptions to what short and tall competitors may do.

### Specialty Elbows

Occasionally Muay Thai fighters launch "specialty elbows." The first and perhaps most common of the specialties is the spinning back elbow. To perform this strike the attacker places his left foot outside the opponent's left leg. The fighter spins clockwise 180 degrees and then strikes with the elbow. The right foot does not step or move forward. The right foot simply pivots in the same place as the fighter spins around.

There are three angles of attack for the spinning elbow: horizontal, upward angle, or downward angle. Regardless of the angle, the spinning back elbow is very powerful.

It is exceedingly dangerous for a fighter to turn his back in a Muay Thai fight. The spinning back elbow is used sparingly and carefully because of this risk. It is sometimes used when an opponent is on the ropes or in the corner of the ring with no room to back away. It must be executed quickly.

Fighters usually set the spinning back elbow

up with a combination attack. Sometimes fighters use the momentum of a missed kick to carry themselves around into an explosive spinning elbow strike. They may also take advantage of a missed jab to spin around and attack the opponent on his left side.

The climbing elbow is another specialty. In this attack one fighter rushes forward and steps on the opponent's thigh. He climbs upward and then drops off, landing the elbow on the head with tremendous downward force.

The flying elbow also strikes downward. It is the only elbow attack initiated from kicking range. To do it, a fighter leaps toward the opponent. The fighter's attack trajectory is forward and up for this technique. The fighter attempts to land the elbow on the top of the opponent's head with maximum momentum. Obviously this is a powerful blow; it is also very risky to the attacker. Going airborne is a major gamble in a Thai bout.

Still the flying elbow can work because it is rare and therefore very surprising to the defender. Villalobos recommends it when an opponent is on the ropes and totally out of gas.

The "invisible elbow" is another sort of specialty. Basically it is the same upward elbow technique commonly used. The things that set it apart and give it the unique quality of invisibility are the angle and timing of its use. It is used at

the hips. The defender may grasp the neck with the left hand and slip in an elbow strike to the clavicle area with the right.

The ear-strike elbow is a particularly tricky elbow. This one is thrown from the clinch. Fighters hold their opponent with both arms and sneak some space between one of their elbows and their opponent's face. Then they snap the elbow in across the ear and jaw. The ear-strike elbow is powerful, fast, and very hard to see coming.

The least common elbow used in Thai boxing is called a spearing elbow. It is done in a close-range position by grabbing the back of the opponent's neck and then driving the elbow in with a straight, spearing thrust. This strike is usually aimed at the eye or the nose. It is extremely rare perhaps because it is easily fended off.

## UPPER-BODY DEFENSE TECHNIQUES

A fighter is vulnerable to counterattack any time he throws a kick, knee, punch, or elbow. To attack, one must break out of the guard position. Throwing any strike requires a variation of balance and therefore puts the fighter at risk. Depending on the technique, the fighter is vulnerable in one way or another. When punching, for example, a fighter is particularly vulnerable to kicks and knee strikes.

Primary defense can be broken down into a small number of options. The fighter can move out of the way, parry, shield, or neutralize by beating the attacker with a faster attack. He can also do any of these primary defensive actions in combination with any number of counterattacks.

Consider, for example, the defensive possibilities when an opponent throws a left jab. The defender can move his head to the side or back to avoid the punch. He might use his left hand to parry the jab with a small circular motion. A third option is to beat the opponent to the punch by firing a foot jab or round kick into his stomach before he can land the jab. The jab is very fast and is typically used to test an opponent. Because it is so quick, it is difficult to respond with a combination. Shielding or moving away is the most common defense for the jab.

The right cross, on the other hand, has more power and a longer flight path. It is relatively easy to respond to this technique with a counterattack. One can, for example, counter with a punch,

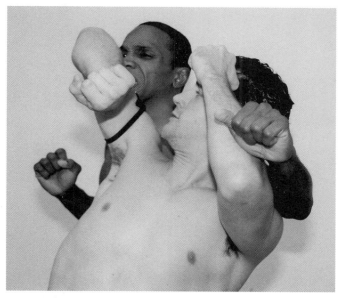

Villalobos uses a spinning back elbow to the body and face to fend off a left kick.

clinch range from inside the opponent's guard. Normally it travels at a 45-degree angle upward. Fighters set it up closing in and touching both gloves to the opponent's gloves. This creates the illusion that the attacker cannot throw an elbow, when indeed he or she can. Further, it serves to limit visibility creating the invisibility effect.

Elbows can also be used to strike the body and the legs. For example, a fighter might grab an opponent's leg and blast it with an elbow. Or one fighter may clinch another by grabbing around

Villalobos stops his opponent's jab with the tip of his left elbow.

knee, elbow, knee, or kick. Or a fighter can simply parry with the left and counter with a right cross of his own.

As with the jab, the first best option to fend off the cross or any punch is to let it miss. Fading back and away from the oncoming fist accomplishes this. Shielding oneself, and then responding with a quick counterpunch or counterkick, is the second most common response.

Thai boxers don't bob and weave much when defending. They are far more likely to pull back or fade to the side than they are to duck under a

Villalobos defends himself against a right cross by parrying it down and preparing to throw a right downward elbow.

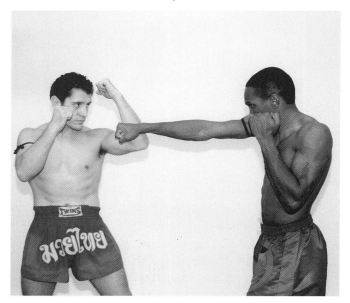

Here he defends himself against the cross with a left elbow parry.

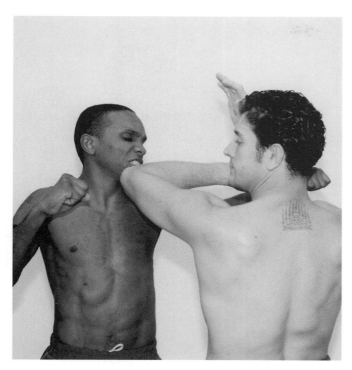

Villalobos defends himself against a left hook with a left elbow.

shield upon which the hooking arm will crash. Thai fighters may turn their elbows to cause damage to the incoming punch.

Against the hook, as with all attacks, the defender looks to counter before the attacker can recover. Common counters to the hook include shielding and then answering with a knee to the stomach or an elbow to the head. Villalobos favors a left hook-right cross-left knee combination when facing a hooking punch.

Hooks enter at a wide angle and are especially effective because they are hard to see. They reach around the guard and therefore require keen awareness and good timing to block. Techniques for fending off both left and right hooks are the same. The first option is to move the head backward and let the attacker miss; this is typically followed by a rapid counterattack, such as a right kick.

A second method for defending oneself against a hook is to shield oneself against the blow and then counter. A fighter might also parry a hook and then counter with a right cross-left hook-right knee combination. Since the hook approaches at an angle, it leaves the attacker open to a variety of counterattacks.

An effective way to stop the hook is to raise the tip of the elbow and allow the hooking arm to spear itself. When the right hook comes in, the fighter angles the elbow outward while keeping

punch or kick. Ducking is very risky in a sport that allows hooking the neck and sending the knee crashing into the face. In defense against the left and right hook, therefore, Thai fighters stay upright. Often they fade back to allow the hook to miss. Sometimes they use the arms as a

Here he fends off a low left hook with a right elbow.

The right arm is used here to block a left hook. The tip of the right elbow hits the biceps.

Villalobos defends against a left and right uppercut by arcing his body backward.

his left glove near his eyebrow and his chin down. The shoulder rises to add protection. Serious damage to the attacker may result when his wrist hits the tip of the defender's elbow.

Uppercuts are even harder to see coming than hooks. Thai fighters keep their bodies straight and avoid resting their weight forward. They do this because putting the weight too far forward creates an arc with the head at the top. A fighter in this position is particularly exposed to an uppercut attack and low-kick attack because his weight is on the front leg.

The first defense against an uppercut is to move back and let the opponent miss. A counterattack of elbows, knees, kicks, and punches is a likely response. A second way to defend against the uppercut is to move into clinch range before the uppercut is released. The opponent cannot use an uppercut from out of a tight clinch.

The uppercut can also be deflected. One method is to bring the defending arm upward as if the fighter is looking at his wristwatch. Next the fist is turned so that the "watch" faces to the outside. This parry is typically followed by an immediate counterattack such as a combination of an elbow strike and knee.

Shielding can also stop the uppercut. Bringing the elbows closer together when in the guard position does this. The attacker's fist lands on the point of the defender's elbow, which can cause real damage to the attacker's fist. The uppercut can also be disabled by a preemptive foot jab. A quick foot jab that beats the uppercut is a common defense.

The uppercut is harder for the attacker to recover from than most other punches. It is also harder to execute; because of its rising angle and slow recovery it leaves the attacker very vulnerable to elbow counterattacks. Western boxers use uppercuts with great effectiveness, but Thai fighters use them only sparingly. Western boxers, however, do not have to worry about knee and elbow counterattacks.

Defense against elbow strikes is vital to survival in a Thai match. Moving away from an opponent can be enough to fend off horizontal, downward, and upward elbows. The elbow attacks can be also be deflected by slightly adjusting the guard position. And the guard position makes it difficult for the attacker to grab the defender's neck to set it up for the elbow.

Another option for defending against the elbow is to push the opponent's face away with one hand before his elbow arrives. Preemptive knee or elbow strikes can be launched to neutralize an opponent's ability to land an elbow.

Elbows are effective in the clinch; however, a savvy fighter may choose to get in a clinch so tightly that the opponent does not have enough

Villalobos uses the tip of his left elbow to block the right elbow of his opponent.

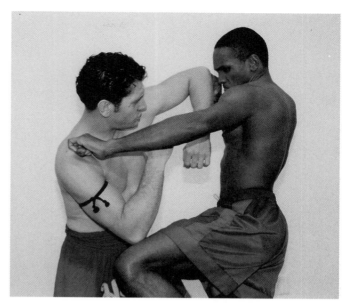

A left-knee attack is countered with a elbow attacks to the face and to the knee.

space to throw an elbow. At this point-blank distance neither fighter can hold a guard position. Knee strikes and throws replace elbows as the weapons of choice in the tight clinch.

The spinning elbow has a lot of power and can be difficult to see. Moving out of the way is a typical and effective defensive response. Normally the defender moves in the same direction as the oncoming attack and causes the attacker to miss. The attacker's back is vulnerable when he turns to throw the spinning elbow. So at this instant, a foot jab or round kick to any number of targets can neutralize the attacker. The spinning elbow can also be shielded against on a closed guard.

Kicks to the upper body and head can be evaded by moving away or deflecting them with defensive kicks and elbows. Thai fighters use the middle and outside part of the forearm to parry high kicks. Highly skilled fighters may try to spike the foot with the tip of the elbow (shielding), causing lots damage and pain to the attacker.

A fighter can dodge high knee attacks by moving backward or sideways. You can also defend yourself against knee attacks by tightening the guard and deflecting them. And high knee strikes can be parried with an elbow. A defender's knee is often used to deflect or shield against an attacking knee. The defensive knee is thrown at the same time and in order to intercept an

incoming knee strike. High knee strikes can also be avoided by simply pushing the attacker away.

With so many weapons and so few rules, the possibilities for attack combinations and defensive responses are virtually unlimited. Thai fighters must be skilled at defense at all ranges. Thai fighters can deliver a knockout or seriously damaging blow at any range. If you were to pull a Thai fighter into a clinch, for example, you would experience the devastation of powerful cutting elbow strikes to the head. A Thai fighter can easily break ribs with knee strikes and then follow up by slamming an attacker to the floor with a leg sweep that hits the knee.

If the attacker manages to stay on his feet and push the Thai fighter away, the latter will likely punch to the face and body before blasting away with knee strikes to the chest and face. If the attacker is still standing, he should expect round kicks to the legs and more triangulated punches to the face. If the attacker tries to get away, the Thai fighter will try to take his head off with round kicks and to break ribs with combinations of round kicks and foot jabs. There is no safe place to be except perhaps outside the ring.

The next chapter continues the examination of the fundamental Muay Thai techniques by outlining the lower-body offensive and defensive techniques.

# 3

# LOWER-BODY OFFENSIVE AND DEFENSIVE TECHNIQUES

nlike other styles that sport six or more basic kicks, Muay Thai has only two: the foot jab and the round kick. Occasionally a Thai boxer will throw a back kick, side kick, or a hook kick in a bout, but each is extremely rare. The foot jab and the round kick are the meat and potatoes of Muay Thai kicking.

There are several reasons why Thai boxers make primary use of only two kicks. First, as discussed in Chapter 1, the Muay Thai art evolved over hundreds of years as a part of the extremely efficient battlefield fighting system of ancient Siam. The descendant of the ancient war arts exists today as krabi-krabong, which emphasizes weapons of all sorts and includes empty-hand techniques, sometimes called Muay Thai Boran or Old Muay Thai. Muay Thai Boran was taught to soldiers in ancient times in response to invasions from neighboring countries. The Siamese armies were composed of rapidly formed groups. The recruits were mostly civilian farmers, and the amount of time available to train them for combat was typically very short. Casualties were high in these old battles. Replacement soldiers had to be drafted and trained very quickly. Resources were scarce, and there was no time for new recruits to master anything fancy or complicated. Thus only the most efficient weapon and empty-hand methods were taught, and only those techniques that proved themselves effective on the field of battle were retained. The front kick and round kick were easy to learn and proved to be especially effective in combat.

Second, Thai boxing allows the use of many body weapons including hands, elbows, knees, shins, and feet. To make best use of these many weapons the body is kept facing the opponent. To defend oneself against these same weapons the body must be also kept facing the opponent. Many kicks (such as side, back, and hook) require a fighter to turn the body sideward. Turning to the side blocks off half of the fighter's defenses and simultaneously exposes him to a whole array of counterattacks on the open side.

Power and speed make up the third reason that Thai boxers rely mostly on only two kicks. The Thai foot jab and round kick have lots of power and are generally faster than anything else that the fighter might consider using. Fourth, round kicks and foot jabs take less energy than many other kicks such as side, back, hook, and ax kicks. Thus a fighter who uses only front and round kicks can last longer in the ring and maintain more power throughout the battle.

The fifth major reason that Thai fighters rely on the foot jab and round kick is defense. It is easier to protect the foot, ankle, and leg when front kicking or round kicking. It is also easier to protect the support leg when using the foot jab and round kick than with other kicking techniques. Recovering the leg is also faster and safer when using round kicks and foot jabs. Thai fighters say they favor foot jabs and round kicks because there is no time or place for fancy stuff in the ring. Everything the fighters use must be quick, effective, defensible, and efficient.

The most common kick seen in Muay Thai matches is the low kick. Legs are fairly easy targets to attack. The leg can only take a few kicks before losing its strength. Seasoned boxers struggle not to show any sign of being hurt if kicked in the leg. Their seasoned opponents will definitely take advantage of any perceived weakness and continue to attack the same leg. If a fighter is hit in the thigh two or three times he is very likely to collapse. The strategy is simple: destroy the leg; if a fighter cannot stand, he cannot fight Muay Thai.

### FOOT JAB

The Muay Thai foot jab is a front kick typically thrown with the leading leg. Unlike front kicks from most other styles, it does not chamber the knee and it does not snap back after impact. According to Villalobos, chambering the knee doesn't work in Muay Thai fighting because it takes too much time, reduces power, and

Short step right footwork on the left foot jab.

telegraphs the fighter's intent. The toes pull back and face up or may face up and slightly to the inside when one does a Muay Thai foot jab. This is to protect the foot from counters launched by the opponent.

The Muay Thai foot jab is quite versatile. It can hit any target from legs to head with damaging force. There are basically four types of foot jabs: the short advancing foot jab, the long advancing foot jab, the hopping foot jab, and a foot jab done after shielding without putting the foot back on the floor. The foot jab is quick, and

Long-step right footwork on left-foot jab.

A hopping foot jab.

because of its angle it is very difficult to see it coming. In fact it is almost invisible. The foot jab usually strikes with the ball of the foot, sending its energy into the target. The energy may go upward, straight ahead, or be triangulated downward depending on the target.

To throw a foot jab, Thai fighters bring the kicking leg up to the height of the hip, lift the knee up a bit, and snap the kick forward using a push with the ball of the foot. The leg extends to complete the kick. It presses through and returns to the floor in a circular motion. It does not snap back.

The energy for the foot jab comes from the ground. It is transmitted from the ground through the toes to the support leg and into the hips. From here, the energy flows into the kicking leg. As with the round kick, the foot jab is expressed with the whole body. The entire body creates the kick, not just the leg. Add good timing, and the formula is complete for a simple and very powerful kick.

The foot jab can be thrown without stepping forward. It can also be launched by taking a step with the rear leg to close the gap or by hopping

Fending off a right-foot jab with a double counterattack of a right knee and right elbow.

forward toward the opponent. If the foot jab is aimed below the waist it includes six energies: gravitation, transition, velocity, a little bit of hip rotation, snap from the supporting foot and knee, and triangulation as it drives downward toward the floor upon impact. The foot jab may reverse-triangulate when thrown at the upper body or head.

The Thai foot jab is slightly less powerful than the round kick. However, the foot jab is a bone breaker in its own right. Done properly and with good timing, the foot jab can knock the wind out of an opponent, break ribs, and even deliver a knockout. Villalobos says the foot jab is as powerful as, and much safer to use than, the side kick and the back kick.

Thai fighters do not normally use side kicks. They claim that turning sideways opens one-half of the fighter's body to counterattack. The support leg is especially vulnerable. The side kicker's ankle is also susceptible to counterattack. A Thai fighter will likely respond to a karate or taekwon do–style side kick by smashing the attacker's kicking ankle between the tip of the elbow and the knee. The rising knee and downward spiking elbow can cause a contusion to the ankle that will result in serious damage and maybe even a technical knockout. The foot jab is far less vulnerable to such a violent counter because the heel is pointing downward upon impact.

Never do a foot jab with the toes pointing

forward. The toes should face upward and curve backward as much as possible. If toes face forward there is a high chance of having them broken by the opponent's elbow. Broken toes are painful, and they take many weeks to heal.

Remember to protect the toes by pulling them backward and avoiding bringing the knee into a high chamber before kicking. Lift the whole leg up, keeping it slightly bent, and in the last moment thrust it forward. This action is safer and much faster than a chambered-knee front kick. In Muay Thai, everything happens quickly, and you need all the speed you can get. If you high-chamber the knee, you will never be fast enough to hit the opponent with a foot jab.

## ROUND KICK

The round kick is the most commonly thrown kick in Thai boxing. The foot jab is second, and the back kick is a very distant third. The Muay Thai round kick is a penetrating kick that can be launched at head, body, and leg targets. Muay Thai round kicks differ from the round kicks seen in most other styles because they attempt to strike the opponent with the lower half of the shin. The shinbone is sharp and hard and makes a formidable weapon. Muay Thai fighters also strike with penetrating power. Their kicks do not snap in and out of the target.

The Muay Thai round kick originates from the

A round high right-leg kick to the neck.

A round right-leg middle kick (close-in and far-away view).

Villalobos fending off the high right-leg kick by arcing his head and body. The top photo shows Villalobos with only the left hand up while the bottom photo shows him with both hands up.

floor: the fighter typically throws it with the rear leg. To attain maximum power and to close the gap on the target, the fighter speeds in and employs transition power by moving forward. Just as with the punching and elbow striking techniques, the fighter will turn his hip and torso to gain rotation.

Most Thai fighters keep the leg relatively straight when round kicking. There is a snapping of the hip as the leg levels out and a drive downward to triangulate energy as the leg makes

contact. Of course, gravitation makes it all possible; thus the Muay Thai round kick employs five or six of the seven powers used in punching and elbow striking.

Sometimes Thai fighters practice round kicks in the open and intentionally spin all the way around. This is done to teach the body to commit full power to the kick. The spin-around drill is just that, however. It is a drill done as an exercise in power and motion. (Fighters do not normally spin around and expose their backs during a match.)

A round low kick.

Top: Blocking a right-leg low kick on the outside.
Above: Fending off or blocking a left-leg low kick on the inside.

The power of the kick and the control of the kick are equally important. When a kick misses the target, the fighter attempts to return to base after the follow-through without spinning. He does not snap the leg back; rather, he follows the energy of the kick downward and returns the leg to base in a circular motion.

Thai round kicks differ from those of other styles. For example, taekwon do and many styles of karate and kung-fu chamber the leg before firing a round kick and snap it back after impact.

The Muay Thai version does not chamber the knee and does not snap back.

When practicing with the heavy bag, fighters visualize their shin's penetrating the target. They imagine, before actually striking, that their leg will pass into and downward through the bag. This visualization allows the mind to direct the motion and the energy of the body, creating amazing power.

It is important to pivot on the ball of the foot when executing a Thai round kick. The heel should be off the floor so that the foot can spin

Grabbing the right-leg round middle kick and counterattacking with a right down elbow.

Top: Defending the kick with a left-foot jab on the opponent's leg.
Above: Blocking a right middle kick with a left knee.

on the ball of the foot with minimal contact with the ground and therefore minimal friction. During a high right-leg kick the right hand drops to add power to the body as it rotates. The hands stay up or push into the opponent's face during middle and low round kicks. The fighter gets transition power by stepping forward, rotation power from the hips when initiating the kick, snap from the supporting foot upon impact, and triangulation power by driving the leg downward upon impact when the round kick is aimed at the waist and lower.

The snapping power generated upon impact is very important to the dynamic of the round kick. Simply spinning on an axis is not enough for Thai fighters, because they seek maximum power. Pushing forward off the ball of the foot adds considerable wallop to the kick upon impact.

The mechanics of the whole round kicking process is very similar to those of a baseball batter at work. As a right-handed batter's body moves toward the ball, he gains velocity and transition power; when his hips turn counterclockwise he gets rotation power. When he makes contact with the ball and surges forward on his left foot he gets snapping power. The extra power provided by the snap, that surging energy from the left foot, may provide the extra power necessary to get a long fly over the fence. When he follows through, allowing the bat to swing around and downward, he adds triangulation energy. Like everything else in sports, gravitation makes it all possible.

Muay Thai fighters target a wide range of areas for their round kicks. The head is a fair target. A solid blow from a full-power Muay Thai shin kick to the head can render an opponent unconscious or indeed cause death. Even at head level the raw power of the Thai round kick is unbelievable.

This round kick is even more powerful lower down. It is aimed at a variety of midbody targets, including the chest, side, stomach, hip, and kidneys. Broken ribs, and even broken arms, are fairly common in Thai boxing.

Leg kicks are usually aimed at the thigh. Just a half-power kick to the thigh can be temporarily crippling. When the sharp edge of the shin drives into the thick meat of the thigh, the nerves are shocked and the muscle bruised. Thai-style thigh kicks are now common in Western kickboxing. Adding the leg kick totally changed the defensive and offensive game for Western fighters. Thai-style leg kicks have also been used very successfully in no-holds-barred competitions. In some cases smaller, faster competitors have used the thigh kick to literally take the legs out from under larger opponents.

Among the many advanced variations of the round kick is the suitcase kick. This is a low round kick that snaps and thrusts downward. This technique makes ample use of the power of triangulation: the effect of a suitcase kick on the leg is devastating. Its only drawback is that it can leave the attacker open to a damaging collision with the defender's knee.

## KNEE TECHNIQUES

There are four fundamental knee techniques in Thai boxing: the clinch knee, straight knee, flying knee, and circle knee. In the clinch, knee strikes fly at a 45-degree angle or straight up, depending on what part of the body the fighter grasps. For a knee to the head, for example, the attacker normally has a clinch around the opponent's neck, and the angle is straight upward. If the fighters are in a very tight clinch, a 45-degree angle is likely and the ribs or legs are good targets. It is common for a fighter to push himself backward while in the clinch to again enough space to throw the knee straight forward or at a 45-degree angle.

The body should be held straight up when throwing straight or 45-degree knee strikes from the clinch. The toes point downward, and the heel should be pulled in tight toward the attacker's body. Energy for the knee strike comes from the toes. Fighters balance on the toes, not on the ball of the foot, at the moment of impact.

The circle knee is also used in the clinch position. It is typically done when the clinch is so close that both the straight and the 45-degree

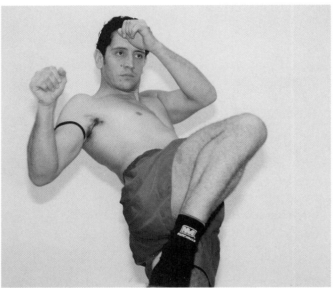

Top: Left knee.
Above: Right knee.

attack angles are blocked. The circle knee swings around in a wide arc and strikes the opponent in along the side of his body. Some fighters let the ankle and the knee hit simultaneously.

The flying knee is done by stepping forward and jumping into the opponent. It is often used when an opponent is on the ropes or in the corner. It is seldom done in the center of the ring. Impact comes when the fighter lands: he drives the knee downward, triangulating power into the target.

Fans of Muay Thai in Bangkok adore knee strikes. The knee is the single most popular

Here Villalobos defends against a right knee by placing his hand on his attacker's chest.

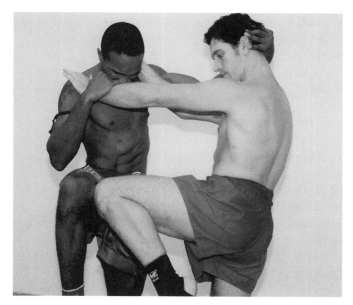

Villalobos defends against the circle knee with a straight knee to the thigh.

weapon, and the crowd tends to go wild when fighters use the knee. The knee is a versatile and very powerful weapon. For example, if a Thai fighter clinches with another fighter who does not know how to defend the knee, he will easily knock the other out in less than 10 seconds. Just two or three knee blows will take a fighter's air away, and one shot to the head can cut or knock an opponent out cold.

Knees are frequently used against the body, with the goal being to knock the air out of the opponent and take his breath away. The body is a bigger and easier target than the head, and Thai fighters know that if they "kill the body the head will die." Knees disable the body and therefore the fighter. It is hard for an opponent to defend or attack when they cannot breathe.

Simply put, all knee strikes to the body hurt. Even glancing shots can result in shocking pain. Fighters are trained to hide their discomfort lest their opponents exploit the injury.

Despite the potential of knee strikes to do serious harm, Villalobos says that Thai fighters do not particularly fear the knee more than punches, kicks, and elbow strikes. Well-trained fighters can defend against knee strikes as well as against strikes from any other weapons.

Thai fighters train knee strikes in a variety of ways, including shadowboxing drills. In these drills a number of footwork patterns are

employed. Shadowboxing has a lot of value: it teaches the fighter fluidity and control of the knee and other body weapons, and it also helps fighters learn to control balance and avoid traveling forward too much when striking with the knee.

## KICK AND KNEE DEFENSE TECHNIQUES

Defense against Muay Thai kicks is a matter of getting out of the way, shielding, grabbing the leg, or striking preemptively. Counterattack is a key feature of all Thai defensive responses. For example, the foot jab can be avoided by moving back or to the side. The fighter may simply arc backward just enough to let the kick miss. The defender usually responds with an immediate counterattack, often featuring round kicks and punches.

The foot jab can be parried with the palm or forearm. Counterkicks to the attacker's support leg typically follow. The foot jab can also be neutralized with defensive shielding. This is done by modifying the guard position slightly as the foot jab comes in. One or both arms and the elbow adjust forward in front of the defender's nose, causing the kick to land on the guard. Shielding oneself against the foot jab can also be done with the knee.

Grabbing the foot or hooking the attacking leg is a versatile defense against the foot jab. For example, a defender may capture the incoming foot and respond with a counterkick behind the attacker's knee. This sweeps the attacker to the floor. Another option is to grab the leg with one hand and punch, elbow, knee, or kick the attacker. There are at least 10 similar leg-grabbing and counterattack techniques Thai fighters use to fend off the foot jab.

Sometimes a fighter preempts a foot jab with another foot jab. For example, if a fighter senses that a foot jab is about to be launched, he may throw a defensive first strike to the other's leg. The effect is to jam the attacker's kick or upset his balance enough to cause him to abort the strike.

One of the most damaging kicks in Muay Thai is the round kick to the thigh. It is a relatively safe kick to throw—and a particularly painful kick to receive. The kicker uses the sharp edge of the lower half of his shin as a weapon. The destructive power of this kick is so great that it can temporarily cripple an opponent.

There are essentially three ways to defend oneself against the low round kick. The first is to step or slide back and allow the attacker to miss. The second is to shield oneself with the same-side or the opposite-side leg. The low round kick is best shielded against with the defender's shin. The defender attempts to use the upper half of his shin to deflect the incoming kick. In this way, the shin as a weapon is used similarly to the Thai krabi-krabong sword. With the sword, the higher part is used for defense, and the lower part of the blade is used for cutting.

Even better than using the upper half of the shin is to shield with the knee. A knee shield can cause serious damage to the kicker's leg. Since the round kick to the leg comes in at thigh level, it is quite practical to shield oneself against it with the tip of the knee.

The middle round kick is a rib breaker. It can be fended off by moving away, shielding, grabbing, or by intercept striking. You can avoid it by stepping or sliding back. It is always good to follow with a counterattack. Shielding oneself with the knee or the upper part of the shin works well against the middle round kick. If a defending fighter attempts to grab the middle round kick, it is important to move with the kick to allow some of its power to diminish first. After grabbing, fighters often follow up with punches, elbows, knee strikes, or leg sweeps. You can

intercept this kind of kick by stepping into it and throwing a series of punches, knees, and or elbows. It is also possible to preempt the middle round kick with a foot jab.

Stepping to the side and moving the head back can work to fend off the high round kick: this causes the attacker to miss. You can also defend yourself by adjusting the guard a bit and allowing the opponent's foot to hit the elbow. This can cause a lot of damage to the attacker's foot or shin. Always follow with an immediate counterattack. Low and middle round kicks are logical counterattack weapons to follow the high round kick.

Knee attacks can be fought off by moving away. In the clinch, however, moving out of the way may be impossible. When thrown from the clinch, the straight knee and the 45-degree knee can easily hit a defender's legs or torso with punishing effect. In the clinch, Thai fighters defend themselves against the straight knee by shielding themselves with their elbows or knees. If the attacker strikes with a straight right knee, the defender will likely respond with a counter knee strike to the inside of the attacker's thigh. This can damage the attacker's leg. The knee attack can also be preempted by throwing a first strike in anticipation of attack.

It is important to stay close and move in the direction that the knee is coming so that the power is less if it penetrates one's defenses. This is true for the straight knee and for the 45-degree knee. Knee strikes are more surprising than they are fast: they are difficult to see coming, especially in the clinch.

The essence of Muay Thai leg attack and defense can be summarized in three words: efficient, powerful, and simple. There is no magic involved in training or conditioning. Basically it boils down to hard work and consistent and correct training.

## FOOTWORK STRATEGIES

Like all martial arts Muay Thai has its own footwork. Unlike many other Asian arts, Muay Thai uses a comparatively simple method for stepping and moving. It is all based on the principles of Muay Thai that include an affinity for simplicity, speed, power, efficiency, and flexibility. Like everything in Muay Thai, the footwork is fast, efficient, and fairly simple. Nothing is wasted. Every motion and every step have a purpose. Balance and fluidity of stance are critical. The ability to deliver and support any body weapon at any time is the key element.

Thai fighters hold their heads high and keep their bodies erect. The head is kept high in part due to the fact that most Thai boxers are Buddhist, and Buddhist tradition maintains that the head is sacred and should be held high. The notion of bobbing and weaving the head lower than that of the opponent is contrary to this important cultural tenet. From a practical standpoint, it is unwise for Thai fighters to lean their heads forward or lower them to evade blows. Knees and elbows are legal weapons in Muay Thai matches, so the likelihood of catching one on the head when bobbing and weaving is very high.

The upright posture is supported by a mobile stance. A right-handed fighter stands with his feet approximately shoulder-width apart, with the left foot slightly in front of the right. The body is open to the opponent, and the weight is distributed evenly between both feet. Keeping the body open and the weight evenly distributed is vital because it allows the Thai fighter to strike with either arm or either foot without readjusting his stance.

Thai boxers stay up on the balls of their feet and shift their weight according to the technique to be applied. Immediately upon completion of any technique or combination of techniques, the fighter returns to the basic fighting stance with the center of gravity exactly between the legs.

Thai boxing footwork is functional, not fancy. Basic footwork does not typically include cross-steps or tricky jigs. Maintaining the integrity of the stance while moving forward, back, side to side, and at angles is a key element.

There are three basic kinds of footwork in Thai boxing: sliding, hopping, and switching. Sliding is perhaps the most common of the three. Fighters move at any angle using the slide. For example, if a right-handed fighter wishes to advance, he steps forward with the left and slides the right. To retreat, he steps back with the right and slides the left. To move to the side or at an angle the same method is employed, step and slide. With each slide the following foot slides quickly back in the basic shoulder-width position.

Hopping is used to deliver flying knee strikes and flying elbow attacks. Hopping attacks commit the body to the air and thus render the attacker especially vulnerable to counterattack. Because of this liability, hopping is rarely applied in the center of the ring. It is commonly used to deliver a specialty attack against an opponent who is on the ropes.

Switching is an enormously important footwork technique in Thai boxing. Assume that a right-handed fighter faces his opponent with the left foot forward. To switch, he instantly changes his lead side. In other words, after switching, his right foot is forward of his left.

Switching is opportunistic footwork. Fighters do not switch sides for the fun of it. Thai boxers do not normally use switching to move toward or away from an opponent; this is valuable only in certain situations. For example imagine that a fighter is defending himself against an aggressive fighter. The aggressive opponent moves in rapidly and closes off the defender's right side, and the defender sees an opening on his left. Rather than back away, the defender switches quickly and round kicks the aggressive fighter's thigh with his left shin. In effect, the defender has created space needed to kick the aggressive attacker without moving back.

Thai footwork is practical and efficient. Perfecting it takes time, and Thai masters require their students to practice a number of special footwork drills. One of the most commonly seen in Thai camps is the "wheel." Trainers use a real tire from a tractor for this drill. The flat tire is placed on the ground, and the boxers proceed with a series of footwork transition drills. They jump up and down on the sides of the tire and switch left and right in rapid succession. When the trainer commands, they flow from north to south or left to right. The wheel footwork drills are great for balance and cardiovascular conditioning.

Thai footwork varies slightly when the fighters are at different ranges. For example, switching is typically used only at very close range. Much of the footwork is actually in turning the foot, as in the example of delivering a hook or lateral elbow. The posture remains essentially intact, but the foot turns to bring energy to the hip and upward for triangulation.

There are many variations on Muay Thai stance, and all are correct. Think of them as style variations or personal preferences. Often an individual fighter develops a unique stance or specialized footwork that takes advantage of a particular skill or natural ability.

When an opponent throws a round kick, for instance, evade it and then close the gap with a fast sliding step. The cross is a good counter when the fighter uses sliding to position the body correctly. The main thing is to move to a point that allows you to control the opponent's centerline. The goal is to slice through the opponent's center of gravity and punch. If you do this, your punch will have maximum effect.

You can also use the sliding step to beat an opponent to the punch or kick. For example, if an opponent prepares to kick, you can neutralize the attack by sliding in and throwing a preemptive foot jab or round kick. You can also slide in and neutralize the attack with a cross. The trick is to use footwork to gain position to control an opponent's centerline. The objective is to slide in and slice through the opponent's center of gravity.

Using sliding footwork to beat the other guy to the punch requires great timing. This comes from lots of Thai pad practice and sparring. You must learn to sense the opponent's intention before he is launched and then time the footwork to gain a first-strike position. The goal is to beat him to the punch and, if that is not possible, to sideslip the punch or kick. Remember to take short steps because they are much faster and a lot safer. Use sliding footwork to get in and out of range very quickly. It is better to take several steps to cover ground when sliding than to take big steps. Big steps move the center of gravity too much and expose the legs to attack.

Hopping works well to close the gap between you and another fighter. The hop is fast and difficult to defend against. The hop also works well for certain defensive responses. For example, if an opponent kicks, you can parry with the shin and bring the leg to the ground without committing weight to it, and immediately hop forward and launch a counterkick. In this case the hopping footwork adds speed and power to the kick. Done with proper timing it is very surprising and can be devastating.

Use switching only when it provides an advantage. Villalobos teaches his students not to switch stances just for the sake of moving. His method requires the fighter to pick a lead and a follow side and stay with it unless there is a need to switch. Some of the opportunities for switching leads include the strategy of starting a fight with the strong side leading. The idea is to mislead the opponent to make him think that he is dealing with a southpaw. This gives the opponent a false read. In the second round switch to left lead and continue the fight.

Another opportunistic use of switching is that moment in which a back-leg kick misses or is blocked. Rather than reset to the rear position, it may be advantageous to lower it in the front and switch to right lead for the rest of the exchange.

As Villalobos relates, "I saw some fighters switching all the time. It makes you vulnerable to low kicks when you do this. When you switch, your center of gravity moves, and it takes too much time to readjust. I've seen many fights lost from switching. Don't switch for no reason. Each side has its job to do."

## MUAY THAI FOOTWORK COMPARED

The footwork of Muay Thai can be grasped more quickly when contrasted to different styles of fighting. To give the reader a good understanding, let's consider Muay Thai footwork in contrast to the following arts: Western boxing, wing chun, kickboxing, taekwon do, and judo. Each of these fighting styles is effective and proven, and the purpose of this comparison is not to say that one is better than another but rather to illustrate the differences of the Thai approach to footwork.

Although there are some similarities between Muay Thai footwork and that used by Western boxers, the differences are significant. Consider these examples. Thai boxing requires extensive pivoting of the whole body to throw very hard blows. Eighty percent of the Thai fighter's strikes are of high power because he has fewer rounds than the boxer. Thai footwork must enable four different weapons in four different ranges, whereas boxers use only their arms. Thai fighters keep their bodies straight while Western boxers bob and weave a lot.

Thai fighters keep their weight distributed evenly between their feet and advance in this way without committing full weight to the leading leg. This is necessary to avoid being kicked in the leg, something that Western boxers do not have to deal with. Thai footwork is very quick but does not have as much variety of steps as Western boxing. Boxing matches usually last 10 rounds, so boxers have more time to play around with pacing and evasive footwork.

Wing chun is a grounded style. Wing chun fighters keep their heels down, while Thai fighters stay on the balls of their feet. Wing chun footwork is designed to draw energy from the earth. When wing chun fighters punch, they gather energy and push it upward. The result is a powerful, grounded punch. Thai fighters draw energy from the ground too but use their position to triangulate downward. Thai footwork is done to get the fighter in and out rapidly while delivering various combinations.

Western kickboxing has evolved over the past several years and now includes leg strikes. The footwork is becoming more similar but still differs from that of Muay Thai. For example, Western kickboxers use a lot of hip motion, and Thai boxers do not. Western boxers can put more weight on their forward leg because the knee strike is not allowed. Thai boxers move their whole body straight in, whereas kickboxers play a little more with the shoulder and with sideward motion.

Taekwon do fighters typically turn their bodies and fight along one line; Thai boxers keep their stance more open and fight on two lines. Taekwon do fighters tend to use one side of the body; Thai fighters use both sides. Taekwon do's side attacks are quicker than Thai attacks, but according to Villalobos they are less powerful.

"They have less power, because in taekwon do side kicks do not have the weight of the body behind each attack in the way that Muay Thai kicks do," Villalobos says. Footwork is typically more one-dimensional, favoring a straight line and lots of forward and backward movement.

Judo is another very grounded style of fighting. Depending on the teacher, judo fighters may spend about 80 percent of their time in stand-up fighting and about 20 percent on the ground. Footwork is quick and rooted. In judo matches, you see lots of forward stepping and pivoting for position to throw. Where Thai fighters stay up on the balls of their feet, judo fighters stay very low with their legs bent.

In the *Tao of Jeet Kune Do* Bruce Lee wrote, "Moving is used as means of defense, a means of deception, a means of securing proper distance

for attack, and a means of conserving energy. The essence of fighting is the art of moving."

Muay Thai footwork is unique. There are slides, hops, steps, jumps, and switches, with very few occasions in which the basic stance is lost. Thai footwork is based on the principles of keeping the body open so that all weapons can be thrown at any moment and of keeping the weight evenly distributed between the feet to enable instant left and right attack and defense.

Fighters who are used to kickboxing contests that do not allow leg kicks must go through a severe learning curve. It is very common for fighters unfamiliar with leg kicks to be knocked out by these in the first or second round. It does not take much of this punishment for the new Muay Thai fighter to realize the importance of attacking and defending with the leg.

## THIRTEEN THINGS YOU SHOULD *NEVER* DO WITH THE FEET

1. Step with back foot first when going forward
2. Step with front foot first when going back
3. Cross the feet
4. Keep the feet too close together or too wide apart
5. Place both feet on one line (rather than keeping them on two lines as on a train track)
6. Stand flat-footed when kicking (rather than keeping the heels off the ground)
7. Switch stances for no reason
8. Stand flat-footed
9. Make a big slide when advancing
10. Retreat backward too much because it is a sign of weakness (rather than staying in middle of ring with the left foot in the middle of the ring all the time)
11. Kick without pivoting
12. Change the guard when in an exchange
13. Stand sideways to an opponent

Muay Thai training and conditioning techniques are explored in the next chapter. Muay Thai training is rigorous, to be sure, but it is not brutal. In Thailand, Muay Thai fighters treat their bodies as if they were fine instruments. They constantly tune and condition their bodies with continuous awareness that a healthy and strong body is a must for victory in the ring.

# ④

# TRAINING AND CONDITIONING METHODS

uring his first trip to Thailand, when he trained in at least 45 different camps, Kru Pedro Villalobos experienced a wide variety of living conditions and training facilities. None of the real Thai camps are luxury spots. Some have open-air training areas, and many have concrete floors. A normal camp will have 10 or 12 heavy bags, a Thai boxing ring, lots of gloves, Thai pads, and little else.

The lifestyle of a Thai boxer in Thailand is Spartan. Fighters live in dorms at the camps, which are owned and sometimes operated by promoters. Trainers run the show, and often the wife of one of the staff members does the cooking. You do not enter a Thai camp unless you are absolutely serious about training and fighting.

## THAI CAMPS

Early each morning the Muay Thai fighters assemble for a run. They do this six days a week, unless it rains, every week of the year. It is not unusual to see 20 or more fighters dashing through Bangkok's morning traffic followed by a trainer on a bike. They head out at about 6:45 A.M. and run for at least 40 minutes. On rainy days the fighters substitute jumping rope and other aerobic activities for running.

When the morning run is concluded, the fighters may sip a little coffee, but they do not eat. Training at the camp begins almost immediately after the run. The routines vary somewhat from camp to camp, but a common day includes 20 minutes of skipping rope, 20 minutes of shadowboxing, and a long session of heavy-bag work.

Heavy-bag training is usually followed by an intense session of Thai pad training. Thai pads are thick kicking pads with a leather sleeve to

Top: Villalobos punches the training pads at M. Muang Korn gym in Bangkok.
Above: Villalobos kicking his training partner at the Lanna gym in Chiang Mai in northern Thailand.

Villalobos blocks his training partner's attack and then counters with a foot jab.

secure the forearm and grip handle. The trainer usually holds one Thai pad on each arm. Thai pad drills include practice of the various Thai body weapons. Virtually all training is done in rounds that typically last from 3 to 5 minutes.

The fighters seldom spar. Since the likelihood of injury is very great with heavy-contact sparring, trainers in Thailand use other methods for simulating combat. On average the boxers fight once a month and on rare occasions twice in one month, so that their postfight recovery

period is very brief. Sparring is seen as too risky, as well as detrimental to the healing and fight preparation process.

After the early-morning workout the fighters shower and sit down for breakfast. Thai people eat two meals a day. The Thais are fanatically clean, and Thai fighters are no exception. A fighter never comes to a meal without having taken a shower. It is not uncommon for the fighters to take as many as five or six showers each day.

Villalobos trains at the San Paranekai gym in Ko Samui.

The fighters take a long break after the midmorning meal. They rest or go for a walk. Some camps have televisions. After the break, which may last as long as five hours, the heavy-duty training begins.

### Afternoon Training Session

At most camps the afternoon training session begins around 3:00. It starts with another 40-minute run or comparable aerobic warm-up. On a typical day the afternoon run is followed by serious heavy-bag work. This lasts for some time and is performed in 3- or 5-minute rounds.

Fighters wrap their hands and glove up before tackling the heavy bags. At the same time the trainers prepare for one-on-one work. The trainers wear Thai pads on their arms, thick belly pads, and shin guards. They take one fighter at a time into the ring for two to five 3-minute rounds. During this time the others continue to work the heavy bags.

The trainers allow the fighters to attack them with as much speed and power as they like.

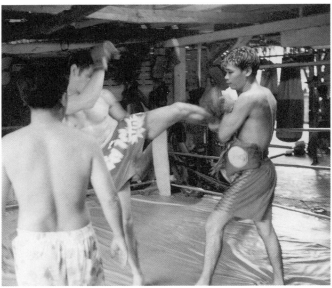

Top: Ajarn Vorapin training a fighter at the So Jorapin gym in Bangkok.
Above: Villalobos kicks a training partner at the So Sritarsri gym in N.S. Thamahat.

Villalobos practicing his kicks at the Lanna gym in Chiang Mai.

Trainers catch every full-contact blow on the Thai pads, belly pad, or shin guards. The trainer moves around the ring like a fighter, forcing the trainee to parry and fake and behave exactly as he would in a real match. The trainer does not hold the pads at certain angles to "ask" for a particular strike. He moves the Thai pads to intercept whatever the fighter throws at him.

This level of training is not for beginners. The trainer must have an extremely high level of skill to absorb every blow the fighters throw, and every fighter is different. In a typical camp one trainer might work with 15 or more fighters. When a new fighter joins the camp, a trainer will work carefully with him for the first three or four days. It takes this long for a skilled trainer to learn the moves of a new fighter. After this careful period of getting to know the new guy, all his Thai pad training will be spontaneous, at full speed and with full contact.

Ring time with the trainer so closely simulates real fighting that it essentially eliminates the need

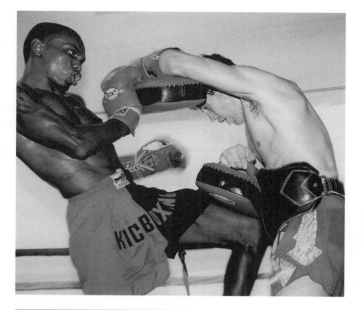

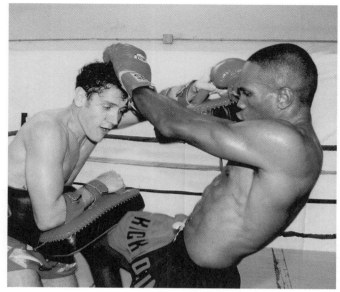

Top: Richard Trammell (on left) attacks Villalobos with his left knee.
Above: Trammell attacks with his left knee while he deflects Villalobos' jab to the side (variation one).

Top: Trammell attacks with his right knee while grabbing the top of Villalobos' head and deflecting his jab down with the right hand (variation two).
Above: Trammell grabs Villalobos' round kick and prepares to attack with the right cross.

for sparring. Ring training is completely safe for the fighters and does nothing to put their health at risk for upcoming fights. Ring training is, however, very dangerous for the trainers: one mistake and they could easily swallow an elbow or receive a full-power round kick to the head.

After the ring training and bag training session is over the fighters remove their gloves and hand wraps. Next on their agenda is an exercise called *plam*. The closest translation in English is neck wrestling.

It is legal to fight in the clinch in Thai boxing.

In fact, many of the techniques of Muay Thai are designed to be done in the clinch. Some fighters specialize in clinch fighting; therefore, plam is an essential part of training. It is the closest thing to sparring you will see in most camps.

The purpose of plam is timing and balance. During the plam exercises the fighters pair up and hook one or two hands around each other's neck. Fighters struggle with great energy to unbalance and throw each other to the ground. It is legal to throw another fighter to the floor from this

Top: Trammell defends the round left kick with "left" foot jab (variation one).
Above: Trammell defends himself against Villalobos' left kick with a "right"-foot jab (variation two).

Top: Trammell attacks with the right knee.
Above: Villalobos attacks with a left high kick, and Trammell counters with a cut kick.

position in a regular match. Fighters also throw knee jabs at each other during this exercise but never at full power.

The afternoon training session ends at about 7:00. The fighters grab another shower and enjoy a bit of free time before their 10:30 evening curfew, which is strictly enforced. Although they are free for a few hours in the evening, there is really very little time for socializing. (Women are not allowed inside a male Thai camp.) Thai boxers follow this routine six days a week.

Everything they do is closely monitored as they maintain the highest readiness for fighting.

In a typical month the fighters will have one match each. To prepare for these matches each fighter, with the guidance of the trainer, follows a proven process for fight preparation. Villalobos calls this the "volume and intensity training cycle."

Imagine a fighter participating in the same daily routine described above. This particular imaginary fighter, however, is recovering from a

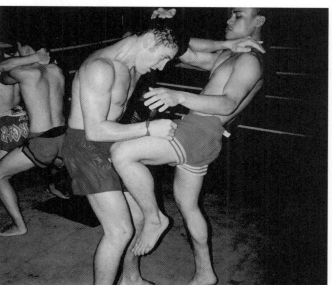

Top: Villalobos grappling at the M. Muang Kom gym in Bangkok.
Above: Villalobos in a clinch at Lanna gym in Chiang Mai.

Top: Villalobos demonstrating the plam in Lanna gym.
Above: M. Muang Kom gym in Bangkok.

fight. For a few days he rests. When he returns to train he starts with more rounds of everything described above but with less intensity. Each day leading up to his next fight, he gradually reverses the volume and intensity formula until he is training with fewer rounds and very high intensity just before the next fight.

Thai boxing is an art and a sport. For those who live and train in professional camps, it is a business as well as a way of life: many fighters begin their training as children. Thai boxing is so grueling and

intense that the oldest professional fighters are in their late 20s or perhaps very early 30s.

## FIST TRAINING AND CONDITIONING

Muay Thai fighters do a lot of knuckle push-ups, and some work with light weights to strengthen the wrist. Since Thai boxers fight in gloves with hands wrapped, however, conditioning the knuckles is not a priority. Knuckle conditioning is not nearly as important

The Wat Ket gym in Chiang Mai.

This Thai youngster demonstrates the plam at Chitrada gym in Bangkok.

in Muay Thai as it is in such fisted arts as wing chun, taekwon do, and karate.

In Thailand virtually all fist training is done with Thai pads. In other countries trainers often use focus mitts on each hand. Villalobos frequently uses one Thai pad and one focus mitt to isolate specific techniques. Speed bags are seldom used in Thailand. A square, wall-mounted bag designed to catch hooks and uppercuts is common in the Thai camps.

The heavy bag is also used for punching techniques and routines. As with most Muay Thai training the techniques are practiced in rounds of 1 to 3 minutes with a rest in between. Typically the period of work is three times longer than the recovery time. Standard punching combinations practiced on the heavy bag include the following and are repeated at high speed for the duration of the round: (1) jab, cross, hook; (2) cross, hook, uppercut; (3) jab, hook, cross; (4) jab and cross; and (5) cross and hook.

Villalobos considers focus mitt training to be very effective for developing punching skills. Typically, the trainer starts with both mitts held to his chest. He brings his left hand up to call for a jab. He brings his right hand up to ask for a cross. If he puts his left hand at an angle to his right shoulder, he wants a left hook. If his right arm faces his left shoulder, he is asking for a right hook. When the trainer's mitt faces the floor in front of his face, he wants the uppercut. All cues are visual; the trainer does not verbally call for punches.

Sometimes the trainer attacks the fighter with the focus mitts and then repositions them to "ask" for specific counters. For example, the fighter throws a jab and cross. The trainer might see an opening and tap the fighter's head with his left focus mitt and then put his right hand at an angle to ask for a hook as a counter. This interactive type of focus mitt training increases speed and timing and develops defensive and counteroffensive skills very rapidly.

## ELBOW TRAINING AND CONDITIONING

Focus mitts may also be used to train elbow skills. Often the elbow techniques are practiced in combination with punches. This is because throwing more than one elbow strike in a row leaves the attacker open to counter. Sometimes the trainer holds both mitts against the fighter's elbows. He taps one elbow or the other to ask for a strike, thus training the student in shielding and counterattacking techniques and reflexes.

Thai pads are the primary tools for training in elbow attacks. There are countless variations mostly involving combinations of punches, knees, kicks, and elbows. As when using the focus mitts, the trainer calls for specific techniques by positioning the pads rather than by asking verbally. Thus the practice sessions are rapid, of full power, and reflexive, and closely simulate combat.

## SHIN AND LEG TRAINING AND CONDITIONING

The shins must be conditioned for Thai boxing. The process of toughening knees, shins, elbows, feet, and fists cannot be rushed. Some Western fighters attempt to rush the conditioning process by pounding their shins into trees or other objects. Villalobos never saw a fighter use these risky methods in Thailand.

Two views of Trammell attacking the pads with a right middle kick.

Muay Thai boxers use their shins as weapons. Virtually all the Thai fighters in Thailand have bumpy, callused, and hardened shins. Professional Thai fighters condition their shins gradually by striking heavy bags and Thai pads and by actually fighting. Thai fighters kick heavy bags and Thai pads hundreds of times every day, and over time their shins become desensitized. The Thai professions also fight one time per month on average. Their shins take a lot of hits during a regular fight, and this adds to the overall conditioning. No additional action beyond bag work, pad work, and regular fighting is required to toughen the shins. Bashing the shins with bottles or kicking trees is unproductive and can damage the fighter's legs.

## THAI PAD WORK

Thai pads are thick pads that strap onto the forearms. They come in different sizes but generally cover the entire forearm. Thai pads are light enough to hold for long periods of training time. They are also thick enough so that when handled correctly they can absorb the most powerful of kicks.

Thai pads are held in place with two straps, one on the forearm and the other on the wrist. There is a grip for the hands; the thumb stays on the outside of the Thai pad. For training, two pads are often used and may be held together to absorb one powerful kick or apart to catch two different types of strike. Thai pads are versatile and can be used to absorb kicks, knee strikes, elbow blows, and punches. There are at least three standard types of Thai pad: extra-long pads, extra-thick pads, and extra-small pads. Each has its specialized purpose in training.

The design of the Muay Thai pad is simple. The pads are rectangular and designed to cover part or all of the forearm. At the top of the pad is a handle. The two straps are attached above the handle. The straps may be buckled or of Velcro depending on the maker. Usually pads are made of leather or leather composite.

According to Villalobos, Thai pads are the best training tool the Muay Thai art has. He says that you simply cannot substitute anything else to develop timing, footwork, technique, and form. Pad work is fabulous for cardiovascular conditioning.

A fighter can work all the Muay Thai body weapons with the Thai pads, including kicks, punches, elbow, knee, and clinch techniques. In Thailand, trainers use the pads for everything. In the West, trainers sometimes use a pad on one arm and a focus mitt on the other hand.

The pads are used to catch all weapons but not always to catch every technique. For example, Villalobos does not use Thai pads to catch leg kicks. He observed that this is seldom done in Thailand because it develops a bad habit for the trainer. Recall that every position used by

Villalobos blocks the right low kick with his left shin.

the holder of the pads is also a real fighting position. Thus it is not good for the holder to use the pads in ways or at angles that do not foster good form.

Villalobos advises the following:

Never hold the Thai pad down. It is a bad habit. First, it is a dangerous and an improper defensive position. If the guy throws a low kick and then a high kick, for example, you will be totally exposed to a knockout if you hold the pads down low. How you place the Thai pads for training is how you fight. Holding the pads is also training the holder how to fight. If you can hold the pads properly, you can fight Muay Thai. It is improper form to drop the pad down to the leg. If you are good at holding the pads, then you understand the mechanics of the motion of the body.

It is also dangerous for the holder to catch leg kicks on the pads. Consider that the holder must turn the elbow out to do this. This puts the holder's elbow at risk. Trainers in Thailand use a special floor-length pad to catch leg kicks. This specially designed pad goes from the floor up and is held by the trainer close to his own leg.

Villalobos trains students past a brief beginner stage by using Thai pads without

Top: Here, the person holding the pads (Villalobos) for the kicker attacks with a right high kick.
Above: As Villalobos attacks, Trammell arcs his body and head back to avoid contact.

Top: As Villalobos kicks, Trammell blocks.
Above: Villalobos kicks with a "round left," and Trammell undercuts his support leg.

verbally calling for a technique. For more advanced students he uses the pads in combination with leg pads, belly pad, and headgear in free form. At this level students throw whatever techniques they like, and Villalobos catches them on the pads. This training is exactly like a real fight but with no risk to the fighter.

Proper technique for holding the pads is critical. When the fighter throws a front kick, the pad holder places one pad on top of the other. For round kicks the pads are held together and at

a small angle or triangle on one side or the other depending on the direction of the kick. It is important to push into the strike upon impact. Otherwise the force of the strike can collapse the frame of the arms, causing injury to the holder. It is really easy to get hurt this way. For example, Villalobos once accidentally broke the ribs of a fellow student who held the pads incorrectly. For safety, the holder must push into the kick.

When catching punches on the Thai pads, you should hold them in front of the body at an angle of

Top: Grabbing Villalobos' left round kick, Trammell is in position to punch.
Above: Trammell grabs Villalobos' left kick from underneath and can then either throw or sweep him.

Top: Here Trammell grabs Villalobos' knee from the top, putting him in a position to sweep Villalobos from the back of his knee.
Above: Trammell demonstrates how to knee the pad with the right knee.

about 45 degrees. Fighters should place the pads so that they face each other a bit. For catching the hook, hold a pad at about a straight-up 90-degree angle. For uppercuts put the face of the pad downward.

To catch knee strikes on the Thai pads, trainers extend one hand with the pad facing down at stomach height and put the pad forward pointing to the other's face. Remember when the knee is coming in, you should push the pad into the blow. This is true for all strikes. It is similar to

catching a baseball—baseball players reach to the ball with their glove. It is important to meet all strikes (including punches, elbows, knees, and kicks) with the Thai pad.

With all the pad techniques the fighter and the trainer should move around. The trainer moves a lot, and the fighter moves to engage. This is vital: it uses the footwork and motion used in real fighting.

An infinite number of Muay Thai pad routines

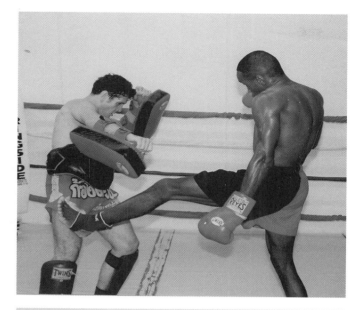

Top: As Villalobos executes a right cross, Trammell defends himself with a left foot jab to his right leg.
Above: Villalobos demonstrates how to work the foot jab to the face on the Thai pads.

Top: Villalobos attacks with a right knee to the stomach.
Above: Here he demonstrates attacking with alternating right and left knees to the body.

is possible. Strive to practice good form and fluidity. Include combinations with kicks, elbows, and punches, as well as those using all the weapons. Fighters must be sure to cover everything in their training and ask for lots of feedback from trainers and training partners. It is good to go fast, but you should also go slow with great attention to details. As a general rule, when training with the pads you should use less power and focus more on perfecting form.

## Basic Routines

1. Round kick at stomach and head level; round kick in doubles at stomach and head level
2. Round kick with speed 10 times in a row with the impact points going up and then back down the torso
3. Trainer kicking and fighter shielding and then returning kick with exact timing
4. Foot jab followed by two round kicks

5. Jab, cross, knee, and elbow strike
6. Roundhouse kick right, switch and double roundhouse kicks left
7. Clinch and knee strike 10 times; then pushing away and kicking
8. Jab, cross, uppercut left, uppercut right
9. Jab, cross, elbow left, elbow right, clinch, knee, break, round kick to the stomach

### Fundamental Rules

While the number of combinations is unlimited, there are fundamental rules that Villalobos believes should not be broken. Here are the top 10 most common mistakes that students and trainers make when working with Thai pads.

1. Holding the pads incorrectly so that the blow gets through to the trainer's body.
2. Not putting energy into meeting the kick. This causes the energy of the kick to bounce into the trainer.
3. Staying still and not moving around. In a fight every thing is moving, footwork. Stationary pad work is not good. In a real fight the opponent is not going to stand still and take it.
4. Holding the pads at improper angles. Otherwise both trainer and fighter will be cheated. If the pads are held wrong the trainer learns incorrect defensive positions, and the fighter learns incorrect angles of impact. Additionally, the energy of the strike will be all wrong.
5. Calling out the technique. The person holding the pads should not say anything. The person kicking should be free to throw any combination. The exception is for new students; after about a month, however, there should be no verbal order to perform a technique.
6. Not attacking. The holder needs to attack as well as defend. Counterattacks, footwork, and aggressive and defensive movements are practiced.
7. Not having time limits. Training with the pads is best done in rounds. Typically rounds last 1 to 3 minutes, and the rest period is one-third of the length of the round.
8. Holding the pads down. This puts the elbow at risk and teaches the holder the bad habit of lowering his guard.

The Muay Thai stance.

### SPARRING

Most of the Muay Thai camps that Villalobos visited did not use heavy-contact sparring as a part of their regular training. They relied on the simulated combat experience described above, in which the trainer wears Thai pads, body pad, headgear, and shin guards. Villalobos does pad training too, of course, but he has also added heavy-contact sparring to his weekly routines, based on his personal belief that sparring is an important tool in fighter preparation.

Villalobos points out that the professional Muay Thai fighters in Bangkok fight an average of once each month. They are in a constant cycle of preparation and recovery. Full-contact sparring would slow their recovery, so they rely on Thai pad training to simulate sparring. Fighters in the United States have far fewer opportunities for matches and sometimes go months between fights. Full-contact sparring helps Western Muay Thai boxers compensate for the time gap. Fighters at Villalobos' gym spar several times a week; they go 15 rounds at 3 minutes each with a 30-second rest period between rounds. They spar in full contact with shin pads, gloves, mouthpieces, and groin cups. Headgear is optional, and few choose to wear it.

"If you train with headgear you will be surprised and disoriented by the sting of the

**FIGHTING STRATEGIES OF MUAY THAI**

punches when you actually fight." Villalobos says. Headgear reduces the cutting of the gloves, protects the face from becoming bruised, and guards against cauliflower ears, but it does little to protect the fighter from injury to the neck or from concussion. For the most part, beginners wear headgear at Villalobos' gym, and the experienced students and the professional fighters do not.

## HEAVY-BAG WORK

Training on the heavy bag has many benefits for the Thai fighter, including cardiovascular conditioning, body weapon conditioning, technique perfection, improved timing, and increased speed. Villalobos has 12 heavy banana bags hanging in his gym. Students move from bag to bag in timed drills that he named the "circle-of-death" routines.

Each of these dynamic routines is done close in to the bag. For the most part, these exercises emphasize close-range kicks and knee strikes. Students begin by lining up behind the instructor or a senior student. Each person strikes a bag 20 times in a specific way before moving to the next bag.

Students are motivated to keep pace because others are always coming up behind them. The fighter behind is hitting his bag 10 times as quickly as possible, and the pressure to keep up forces everyone to increase his speed and focus full attention on the task.

There are countless combinations that can be used in the circle-of-death bag training process. In a typical circle-of-death routine, each person might hold and hit the bag with knees doing five on the left and five on the right. Or a combination of techniques might be applied in a run through the 12 bags. The basic math is that every person strikes each of the 12 bags 10 times in about 2 minutes. Heart rates are elevated more with this method than almost any training technique that Villalobos knows.

There are four fighting ranges in Muay Thai: (1) kicking, (2) punching, (3) elbow and knee, and (4) clinch. The circle-of-death routines usually focus on the elbow-and-knee and clinch ranges.

Typically, students are required to pass through the circle of death three times, or three rounds, in a single class. These kicking marathons make even the fittest students huff

Top: A let-foot jab on the bag.
Above: A left jumping knee on the bag.

and puff. Should a person fall behind or fail to execute the techniques properly during a run, the instructor will usually pull him out for push-ups or other extra conditioning activity as a reminder to try harder next time.

Since Villalobos has 12 bags in his school, one pass through all 12 yields at least 120 strikes. Regardless of how many bags in the "circle," Pedro recommends a minimum of 100 kicks per circle-of-death round.

Most of Villalobos' circle-of-death routines require the participants to hold the bag or restrain

A right knee on the bag.

Top: A left suitcase low kick to the bag.
Above: A regular low kick on the bag.

it in some manner. These are fairly close-range training skills and are very important because they closely simulate common positions of a real opponent in the ring. Typically, fighters do either a low-, middle-, or high-range striking sequence in a circle-of-death routine.

### Circle-of-Death Routines

Following are five circle-of-death routines. Remember to allow at least 2 minutes and at least 100 kicks per round.

1. Hold the bag. Imagine that the bag is a real opponent and control it at all times. Strike the bag 10 times rapidly with knee blows. Alternate left and right knees. Strike to stomach and head level.
2. Strike each bag with the knees 10 times rapidly, alternating blows at head level and stomach level. Strike with power and speed. Emphasize body position, balance, and precise placement of the strikes. Use arms to control the bag at all times. Move to the next bag and repeat.
3. Control the bag at all times. Strike the first bag with 10 circular knee strikes, alternating left and right. Then move to second bag and do 10 low kicks while controlling the bag with feet and knees. Now move to the next bag and do 10 invisible left and right kicks at close range while holding the bag.
4. Strike each bag 10 times rapidly with the elbows. This routine is actually several in one. In one pass you may strike each bag with a high elbow, alternating left and right. In other rounds you may use a different angle or even mix angles to suit. Remember to control the motion of the bag.
5. Wrap the hands and put on bag gloves. Punch the heavy bag about 20 times very rapidly, alternating jabs and crosses. Move quickly to the next bag and repeat. Using different punching combinations—such as

Villalobos shows the proper way to execute a left down elbow on the bag.

jab, cross, hook or jab, jab, cross—creates variations of this drill. Combinations can also include punching and elbow techniques.

### How to Work the Heavy Bag

When striking the bag with the knees at middle and high levels, hit with the front of the knee, the patella or kneecap. Hit with the side muscles of the knee when attacking with the circular knee strike method. Allow the ankle to strike the bag at the same time. Although most of the energy of the circular knee strike is expelled through the knee, residual or collateral damage can occur as the ankle simultaneously contacts the opponent's thigh. Circular knee attacks are particularly useful against an opponent who stays close and clinches a lot in the ring.

Work the bag applying about 80 percent of total power most of the time. This simulates the pace of a real fight. In the ring, if a fighter gives 100 percent of his energy all the time, he will become exhausted long before the final round. In a match, fighters typically go at about 20 percent of capacity in round one, 50 percent in round two, 80 percent in rounds three and four, and 100 percent to the finish in the fifth round.

Fighters who are new to Muay Thai may find it necessary to work the bag with less than 80 percent of full power until their wind is up and their body weapons are conditioned properly. If shins and knees are not conditioned, a fighter must go lighter and build up gradually. There is no way to rush the conditioning process. Regular training on bags and pads will gradually and thoroughly condition the body and the body's natural weapons.

### Heavy-Bag Training Fundamentals

Heavy-bag work can be extremely helpful or very hurtful depending on how it is performed. The following principles will ensure that maximum results are derived from heavy-bag work.

- Do not allow the bag to move much when striking it. Control the movement with the feet and with the placement of strikes.
- Use proper Muay Thai footwork when working the bag.
- Pace yourself. Work the bag at 80 percent of full power 90 percent of the time. Occasionally apply 90 to 100 percent.
- Relax and do not waste energy. Relax first, then strike hard.
- Consider ways to perfect body weapons and fighting techniques. Seek coaching and never be satisfied.
- Imagine the bag as an opponent who is attacking. Visualize these attacks and position to defend and counterattack.
- Work with the bag, not against it. Do not get violent or crazy when striking the bag. Control effort and emotion.

This last principle is particularly important. Self-injury is very common among new martial artists. Striking the heavy bag with speed and power is serious training. Proper positioning and good technique greatly reduce the chances of injury. Getting crazy with a heavy bag is the same as getting violent with oneself. It is unproductive, unnecessary, and dangerous to horse around with a heavy bag.

### WEIGHT TRAINING

If you want to be a Muay Thai fighter, should you train with weights? The answer is yes; however, there are several considerations. Foremost is the fact that added muscle gives you strength but also increases weight. For the most part, fighters like

Villalobos concentrate on building muscle for the purpose of enhancing strength without growing out of their optimal weight bracket. Since only a limited amount of muscle can be added before crossing the weight-bracket threshold, Villalobos chooses to concentrate on muscles that are especially important to the execution of Muay Thai techniques.

For example, Villalobos says that chest and biceps muscles do little for Thai boxing. His weight routine does not eliminate the chest and biceps work, but he pays more attention to muscles that are more useful to Muay Thai. Muscle groups that Villalobos emphasizes for strength include the following:

- Triceps, which give power to punches
- Quadriceps and calf muscles, which increase kicking power
- Muscles in the back of the neck, which protect the fighter from neck injury
- Shoulder muscles, which enhance hook punches and defending
- Muscles in the body's trunk, which improve delivering power to punches and kicks

Following is Villalobos' actual weight training routine. He sticks with this routine throughout the year with the exception of those times leading up to a fight, at which time he alters the routines somewhat to prepare. Note that this routine is not intended to make muscles grow. The goal is to give the muscles high endurance and high resistance, and to make them stronger but not bigger. Strong, tight, hard muscles with high endurance is the goal.

### Strength-Training Routine

Villalobos says, "Strength training is an important part, but I don't want to put the focus and energy of my training on weights. If I do, the next day I will be tired and sore. Just enough weight training to make me stronger and give me higher endurance is all I want. It is enough."

On Monday, Wednesday, and Friday evenings Villalobos' workouts include weight training. On Monday he uses free weights and machine weights for certain parts of the body, and on Wednesday he does the remaining muscles in the same fashion. On Friday, however, he does a full-body strength routine using his body weight only. His Friday strength workout features such

exercises as pull-ups, sit-ups, and squats, all using body weight only, nothing artificial.

### Tips

Depending on the age of the fighter, it may be desirable to do more or less strength training. It is true, unfortunately, that the human body hits and passes through its muscular peak somewhere in the mid-20s. There are exceptions, but most fighters peak before age 25. After this time, the body begins a very slow decline in muscular strength. Older fighters (i.e., anyone over about 26) can compensate by lifting a bit more weight than their younger counterparts.

Regardless of age, the best sort of weight training for a Muay Thai fighter consists of lighter weight lifted in multiple repetitions. This kind of training creates strength to be sure. The emphasis, however, is on endurance. Villalobos says, "If you want to do Muay Thai, you have to be focused on Muay Thai. Avoid heavy weights. Use light weights and do lots of repetition."

To be sure, lifting weights is a productive form of exercise, and virtually all Western sports make use of it. In general, however, Muay Thai fighters in Thailand do not lift much weight. In part this may be because of limited availability of free-weight and assisted-weight equipment. Another reason is the fact that weight lifting is just not part of the training methodology that has worked so well for so long in Thailand.

Should fighters work with weights to supplement their Muay Thai training? Absolutely. Just keep the focus on strength and endurance rather than strength for strength's sake.

If you are not accustomed to lifting weights it is important to start very slowly and build up gradually. The amount of weight and the number of repetitions performed will change as the person becomes stronger. As a general rule, always use weights that are light enough to press 20 times in a row. At the end of 20 repetitions the fighter should feel a slight burn, but not a burnout. The weight should be heavy enough to challenge but not so much that you cannot finish 20 repetitions.

Lift very slowly using perfect form. Control and coordinate the breath. Villalobos' weight-lifting routine, shown below, emphasizes the muscles most helpful in Thai boxing. It does not, however, neglect any major muscle groups. Remember that muscle groups work in opposition to each other. The body's muscles work together in a system of connections. For example, triceps give power to punches. Biceps don't do much for any Thai boxing technique; mostly they just provide balance to the arm and help a little with returning the punch to the guard. Since these muscles work in opposition to each other, big triceps will not have much power or control unless balanced by equally strong biceps.

The following routine is designed to strengthen all the major muscles. Villalobos puts extra work into those that enhance his Muay Thai techniques. For example, strong latissimus dorsi (lat) muscles help his Thai boxing by making the torso stronger, which is necessary for defense. Abdominal training, lower back development, and lower lat work improve Thai boxing techniques because the middle of the body is important to power because it is the source of rotation power.

All the leg muscles need to be developed with vigor because they support footwork and powerful kicks. Calves are especially important and provide a lot of power to the kick. Villalobos says shoulders are particularly important to the Thai boxer because they provide snap to punches and are needed for powerful clinching. Triceps are for punching, and biceps balance the power of the triceps. Neck muscles must be very strong to protect the neck and spine from injury.

Following is Villalobos' weekly routine for strength training. He does these in the evening after a long day of regular Muay Thai training. He says it is important to do strength training after the regular Muay Thai training is complete. Otherwise, the energy is gone, and the fighter's Muay Thai suffers. Remember, fighters must strengthen all major muscle groups, or they will become imbalanced. Emphasize muscles needed for Muay Thai and work them harder but don't neglect the rest.

Done properly, the following routine should not leave a person sore the next day. If you become sore, assuming that you have allowed yourself build-up time for your weight routines, then you are lifting too much weight. Soreness from weight training slows down Muay Thai progress. So if you are overly sore after weight training, cut back on the amount of weight.

## WEIGHT-TRAINING ROUTINE

### MONDAY
### (40 MINUTES)

| Body Part | Exercise | Sets | Repetitions |
|---|---|---|---|
| Back | Lat pull downs | 3 or 4 | 20 |
| | Rows | 3 or 4 | 20 |
| | Pull-ups (palms forward, hands wide) | 3 | 5 |
| Legs | Squats | 3 | 10 |
| | Leg curls | 3 | 10 |
| | Reverse curls | 3 | 10 |
| | Calf raises | 3 | 10 |
| Shoulders | Military press | 3 | 10 |
| | Military press (wide arms) | 3 | 10 |
| | Military press (behind the head) | 3 | 10 |

### WEDNESDAY
### (40 MINUTES)

| | | | |
|---|---|---|---|
| Chest | Flat bench press | 3 | 10 |
| | Lower bench press | 3 | 10 |
| | Upper bench press | 3 | 10 |
| | Dumbbell flies | 3 | 25 |
| Back | Pull-ups | 2 | 5 |
| Triceps | Lat machine press-downs | 3 | 10 |
| | Dips | 3 | 10 |
| | Push-ups | 3 | 10 |
| Biceps | Dumbbells | 3 | 15 |
| | Bar | 3 | 15 |

### FRIDAY
### (BODY-WEIGHT ROUTINE, 40 MINUTES)

Push-ups   (Variety in series of 25; e.g., flat palms, fingers, knuckles, hands at various widths)

Squats
Dips
Pull-ups
Neck bridge at all angles
Neck with weights at various angles
Abdominals
Stretching

## MUSCLE FOR FIGHTING

Putting on lots of muscle makes a person stronger and gives him an edge on the street. Adding 20 pounds of muscle does not, however, make him a better fighter, technically speaking. To become better at fighting you must increase your skill as a fighter. Muscle is fine, but it is not a shortcut to skill.

Weight brackets are in place to support the principle that fighting skill and muscular strength are two different things in competition martial arts. If, for example, a person weighs 150 pounds and cannot defeat anyone at the same weight, he might grow to 175 pounds by putting on lots of muscle. At 175 pounds this person may be able to beat the 150 pounders but how will he do against the 175-pound crowd? He will be losing again, this time in a higher weight bracket. And so it will go, until the person adds skill to the mix.

The street is the place where size and muscle really do matter. From a self-defense perspective, more muscle is better. If street defense alone is the goal, go for it and build as much muscle as possible. If the objective is competition, it is necessary for the individual to determine his own best weight class. Next he must find his own best balance of strength and weight and stick with it.

## THAILAND ARTS INSTITUTE TRAINING CURRICULUM

Villalobos' students learn Thai boxing systematically. Completing the Thailand Arts Institute six-level curriculum, as follows, takes at least 3 1/2 years. Students finish this development process at different speeds because of many factors, including natural ability, age, health, and hours spent in training.

### Level One

**Time Required**
- 3 months (36 hours minimum)

**Stage**
- Beginning
- *Welcome to Muay Thai—Villalobos*

**Goals**
- Identify the four ranges of Thai boxing

- Become familiar with the body weapons kicks, punches, knees, elbows
- Learn basic application of each body weapon in its proper range

**Mental Aspect**
- Begin to study of the history of Thai boxing

**Techniques**
- Muay Thai walk
- Muay Thai body weapons
- Application of each body weapon on the heavy-bag phase 1
- Application of each body weapon on the heavy-bag phase 2
- Application of each body weapon on the heavy- bag phase 3
- Fundamentals of Muay Thai boxing

**Conditioning**
- Jump rope, 15 minutes
- Push-ups, 100 on the knuckles
- Sit-ups, 200
- Squats, 50

**Sparring**
- One round of 3 minutes
- Second round of 3 minutes

**Cultural and Spiritual Aspects of Muay Thai**
- Special sessions with kru

### Level Two

**Time Required**
- 9 months (108 hours minimum), 1 year's total time training upon completion

**Stage**
- Diamond-cutting stage
*(You are starting to sharpen your weapons. The war will come soon. This is a very physical stage and is one of the hardest. You will need all of your energy to pass through.—Villalobos)*

**Goals**
- Increase endurance
- Understand the four ranges
- Perfect the body weapons
- Learn the footwork variations

*Mental Aspect*
- Continue the study of the history of Thai boxing
- Develop basic Thai vocabulary for training
- Learn about Thailand

*Techniques*
- Skip knee 1
- Circular skip knee
- Invisible kick
- Suitcase low kick
- Foot jab, stepping
- Foot jab, hopping
- Foot jab, with shielding
- Identify the proper targets
- Fundamental combinations
- Continue study of boxing basics

*Conditioning*
- Jump rope, 15 minutes
- Push-ups, 100 (various types)
- Sit-ups, 200 (various types)
- Squats, 50
- Circle-of-death heavy-bag routines

*Sparring*
- Two round of 2 minutes against padded trainer
- One round of 5 minutes against training partner

*Cultural and Spiritual Aspects of Muay Thai*
- Special sessions with kru

## Level Three

*Time Required*
- 6 months (72 hours minimum), 1 1/2 years' total time training upon completion

*Stage*
- Focusing the mind
  (*The mind is the most powerful weapon in your body. Without mental control you will not pass through this level.—Villalobos*)

*Goals*
- Learn Muay Thai strategy
- Begin the process of truly knowing self
- Increase power
- Increase speed
- Gain fluidity with combinations

*Mental Aspect*
- Continue the study of the history of Thai boxing
- Increase general knowledge of Muay Thai
- Increase basic Thai vocabulary for training
- Learn more about Thailand

*Techniques*
- Muay Thai double kick
- Advanced knee techniques
- Advanced elbow techniques
- Defense against low kicks
- Defense against foot jabs

*Conditioning*
- Jump rope, 15 minutes
- Push-ups, 100 (various types)
- Sit-ups, 200 (various types)
- Squats, 75
- Circle-of-death heavy-bag routines, two times through

*Sparring*
- Two round of 3 minutes against padded trainer
- One round of 7 minutes against training partner

*Cultural and Spiritual Aspects of Muay Thai*
- Special sessions with kru

## Level Four

*Time Required*
- 6 months (72 hours minimum), 2 years' total time training upon completion

*Stage*
- The invisible connection
  (*The strength of the body and the power of the mind flow together becoming something very unique, you.—Villalobos*)

*Goals*
- Understand energy
- Gain relaxation
- Increase skills
- Increase endurance
- Learn the psychology of fighting

### Mental Aspect
- Continue the study of the history of Thai boxing
- Learn the geography of Thailand
- Increase knowledge of Muay Thai strategy
- Increase knowledge of the interplay of ranges in Muay Thai
- Increase basic Thai vocabulary for training

### Techniques
- Clinch attack 1
- Clinch attack 2
- Clinch attack 3
- Clinch defense 1
- Clinch defense 2
- Clinch defense 3
- Intermediate Muay Thai combinations
- Intermediate boxing skills
- Kick reaction drills
- Knee reaction drills
- Knee-elbow reaction drills
- Timing reaction drills

### Conditioning
- Jump rope, 20 minutes
- Push-ups, 125 (various types)
- Sit-ups, 250 (various types)
- Squats, 100
- Circle-of-death heavy-bag routines, three times through
- Pull-ups, 5

### Sparring
- Three rounds of 3 minutes against padded trainer
- Two rounds of 5 minutes against training partner

### Cultural and Spiritual Aspects of Muay Thai
- Special sessions with kru

## Level Five

### Time Required
- 6 months (72 hours minimum), 2 1/2 years' total time training upon completion

### Stage
- Humility
  *(Being humble is one of the most precious treasures that we have. Humility is what makes a real warrior.—Villalobos)*

### Goals
- Become a Muay Thai trainer
- Learn about nutrition and metabolism
- Learn more about the spiritual aspects of Muay Thai
- Fight for the first time amateur or professional with at least 3 rounds of 2 minutes each

### Mental Aspect
- Secrets of the fight game
- Motivation
- Winning and losing

### Techniques
- Learn the *ram muay*
- Understand the ram muay
- Obtain the mongkon

### Conditioning
- Jump rope, 20 minutes
- Push-ups, 150 (various types)
- Sit-ups, 300 (various types)
- Squats, 100
- Circle-of-death heavy-bag routines, three times through
- Pull-ups, 10

### Sparring
- Three rounds of 3 minutes against padded trainer
- Three rounds of 3 minutes against training partner
- One 15-minute round of clinch sparring

### Cultural and Spiritual Aspects of Muay Thai
- Special sessions with kru

## Level Six

### Time Required
- 12 months (72 hours minimum), 3 1/2 years' total time training upon completion

### Stage
- Full circle
  *(Students who reach this level will become instructors, but at the same time they will return to the beginning because the end does not exist.—Villalobos)*

## Goals
- Become a Muay Thai instructor

## Mental Aspect
- Teach students the mental aspects of the art

## Techniques
- Teach students the techniques of Muay Thai

## Conditioning
- Coach students through conditioning phases

## Sparring
- Coach students in Muay Thai sparring

## Cultural and Spiritual Aspects of Muay Thai
- Escort students to Thailand and train with them for a minimum of 15 days
- Participate in sacred Muay Thai rituals under guidance of the monks
- Present monks with gifts
- Receive the secrets

## STANDARD MUAY THAI TRAINING ROUTINE

When studying the Muay Thai training routine shown below, recall that there are two types of exercise: aerobic and anaerobic. Both are important in Muay Thai. Aerobic exercises may be defined as exercises that keep a person doing the same thing for a long time at the same pace, such as even running or cycling or hitting the bag at the same pace. Anaerobic exercises are those that push the heart rate up very high, let it fall back down, and then push it up again. This cycle of up and down heart rate provides a kind of endurance necessary for fighting.

Most martial artists have to work or go to school and simply cannot train full time. Understand, however, that the professional Muay Thai boxers are not part-time martial artists. They are full-time fighters, and preparing to go against them requires full-time training. Villalobos is a full-time fighter and martial arts instructor. His normal training schedule is as follows. Recall that his schedule changes when fight day nears.

## STANDARD ROUTINE

### MONDAY
- Warm up and stretch: 3–4 minutes
- Run: 1:00 P.M. 30 minutes or 3 miles
- Shadow box: 3 to 4 hand wraps rounds, one with weights, 5 pounds on each hand, 3 to 4 times week
- Bag, bag gloves: 5 rounds, 30 seconds. Rest, 25; knuckle push-ups 25, or squats 20
- Thai pads (trainer style with belly pads, shin pads, head, Thai pads): 3–4 rounds, 3 minutes, 30 seconds' rest
- Plam (neck wrestling): 15–20 minutes
- Calisthenics: abs, push-ups, pull-ups, neck bridges, neck weight work
- Stretch and finish at 3:30 P.M.
- Free weight and machine weight training: 40 minutes at 8:30 P.M.

### TUESDAY
- Warm up and stretch: 3–4 minutes
- Run: 1:00 P.M. 30 minutes or 3 miles
- Shadow box: 3–4 rounds, one with weights, 5 pounds, 3–4 times week, hand wraps
- Bag: 5 rounds, 30 seconds' rest, push-ups 25, or squats 20
- Thai pads (trainer style with belly pads, shin pads, head, Thai pads): 3–4 rounds, 3 minutes, 30 seconds' rest
- Plam: 15–20 minutes
- Calisthenics: abs, push-ups, pull-ups, neck bridges, neck weight word
- Stretch and finish at 3:30 P.M.
- Evening sprints: 10 x 200 feet or so, uphill— the steeper the better
- Evening bag work in combinations: 3–5 rounds
- Stretch

### WEDNESDAY
- Warm up and stretch: 3–4 minutes
- Run: 1:00 P.M. 30 minutes, 3 miles
- Shadow box: 3–4 rounds, one with weights, 5 pounds 3–4 times week, hand wraps
- Bag: 5 rounds, 30 seconds' rest, push-ups 25, or squats 20
- Thai pads (trainer style with belly pads, shin pads, head, Thai pads): 3–4 rounds, 3 minutes, 30 seconds' rest

- Sparring: 15 rounds 3 minutes, 30 seconds rest (1 hour) shin pads, bag gloves, mouth piece, cup. (No headgear—you are going to get hit so get used to it. If a fighter trains with headgear he will be surprised by the sting of the punches when they actually fight. This will disorient the fighter. Headgear, according to Villalobos, does little to protect a fighter from injury to the neck or from concussion. Headgear mostly reduces cutting by the gloves and protects the face from bruising. Beginners wear it. Professionals mostly put it away.)
- Calisthenics: abs, push-ups, pull-ups, neck bridges, neck weight work
- Stretch and finish at 3:30
- Free weight and machine weight training: 8:30 P.M. for 30–40 minutes

### THURSDAY
- Warm up and stretch: 3–4 minutes
- Run: 1:00 P.M. 30 minutes or 3 miles
- Shadow box: 3–4 rounds, one with weights, 5 pounds, 3–4 times week, hand wraps
- Bag: 5 rounds, 30 seconds' rest, push-ups, 25, or squats, 20
- Thai pads (trainer style with belly pads, shin pads, head, Thai pads): 3–4 rounds, 3 minutes, 30 seconds' rest
- Plam, 15–20 minutes
- Calisthenics: abs, push-ups, pull-ups, neck bridges, neck weight work
- Stretch and finish at 3:30 P.M.
- Evening sprints: 10 x 200 feet or so, uphill—the steeper, the better
- Evening bag work in combinations: 3–5 rounds
- Stretch

### FRIDAY
- Warm up and stretch at 1:00 P.M.
- Run hills
- Shadowbox uphill
- Pads on hills
- Calisthenics: abs, push-ups, pull-ups, neck bridges, neck weight work
- Meditate: lotus position, relax, breath deep (see Villalobos' 8-week class routine from temple class); finish early
- 8:30 P.M. body-weight strength training: 30 minutes, light

### SATURDAY
- Run
- Shadowbox: 1–2 rounds
- Sparring: 15 rounds, 3 minutes, 30 seconds' rest (1 hour)
- Calisthenics: very light

### SUNDAY
- Rest
- Go to the mountain
- Walk trails 5–6 miles up and down
- Sometimes fast all day
- Relax

---

Use the chart on page 63 to schedule Muay Thai training by the week. Consistency is the key.

## STRATEGIC FIGHT PREPARATION

It is wise to learn as much about an opponent as possible before facing him in the ring. Many times, however, it is not possible to observe the opponent before a fight. To deal with the uncertainty, Villalobos visualizes the unmet opponent, imagining the person as being bigger, faster, stronger, and more technical than he is. By visualizing himself defeating this "perfect" opponent, Villalobos gives himself a psychological advantage. Invariably, the real opponent does not measure up to the super fighter that Villalobos conjures up.

It is common for Muay Thai fighters to undergo severe preparations in the final few days before a match. In addition to the increase of intensity in training, many fighters seek to drastically reduce their weight. The goal is to drop down one, two, or even three weight brackets in the short time remaining before the battle. This is not a particularly healthy practice, but it is very common.

Consider a fighter whose normal weight is 165 pounds. At this weight, the fighter is considered a middleweight. In this example, however, the fighter will drop from 165 pounds to 154 pounds in just 4 days, thus skipping a bracket and qualifying as a super welterweight. The trick is to lose enough weight to qualify without losing muscle mass or getting sick. This means the fighter must almost, but not quite, starve himself.

| PERSONAL MUAY THAI TRAINING SCHEDULER | | | | | | | |
|---|---|---|---|---|---|---|---|
| | Monday | Tuesday | Wednesday | Thursday | Friday | Saturday | Sunday |
| Warm-up, stretch | | | | | | | |
| Run 30 minutes | | | | | | | |
| Shadow box | | | | | | | |
| Heavy bag | | | | | | | |
| Thai pads* | | | | | | | |
| Plam** | | | | | | | |
| Sparring | | | | | | | |
| Calisthenics | | | | | | | |
| Weight training | | | | | | | |
| Body weight training | | | | | | | |
| Sprints | | | | | | | |
| Stretch, second session | | | | | | | |
| Bag work, second session | | | | | | | |
| Meditate | | | | | | | |

\* Pad work means full-range exchanges done in rounds in which the trainer wears belly pad, shin pads, helmet, and holds the Thai pads for the fighter. This is free form and full contact, and it simulates actual fighting very realistically.

\*\* A form of neck wrestling in which fighters try to throw each other while sparring lightly.

Without food, the body goes into radical starvation mode and shuts down systems to reduce energy consumption. Thai boxers don't have much body fat, so starvation dieting puts them at immediate risk for muscle loss. What they seek to do is rapidly dehydrate themselves without allowing the body to burn into the muscle. This requires a careful balance of an absolute bare minimum of calories to maintain the muscles while the body dries out. As weigh-in time approaches, a fighter will accelerate the dehydration process, if necessary, by wrapping himself in plastic and sitting in a hot sauna.

Losing 10 or 11 pounds of water weight in 3 days is very painful and really hard to do. It takes a massive amount of willpower. Villalobos says he gets so hungry on the last day that when he brushes his teeth he wants to eat the toothpaste. If done correctly, however, it can provide a tremendous advantage in the ring. Consider the example of the 165-pound fighter who lost 11 pounds of water weight in 2 or 4 days. On the day before the fight he weighs in at 154 pounds and qualifies for super welterweight.

Immediately after weigh-in, he begins eating and drinking moderately and almost continually for many hours. His body is rehydrated to its normal weight within 3 or 4 hours. After weigh-in the fighter rests and relaxes to conserve energy and allow his body to readjust. Thai fighters stop eating and drinking about 3 hours before the match. The stomach must be empty of food and water during the fight to avoid the risk of injury.

If all goes well the fighter steps into the ring weighing close to his normal 165 pounds. Since he was careful to balance his calorie intake to avoid muscle loss, his rehydrated body has full muscular strength and a significant size advantage. He has this advantage unless, of course, his opponent did the same thing.

A trainer in Thailand recommended this rapid water-weight loss method to Villalobos as a method of gaining advantage by dropping down one to three weight divisions and still remaining strong. The trainer said, "You hurt and pay the price now by losing the weight so quickly, but when you fight you will be like a giant."

The cost of crash water-weight loss can be the fight itself. Villalobos learned this lesson during his first trip to Thailand when he undertook an extreme water-weight loss of 17 pounds in only 3 days. This is how it went in his own words:

I was training at a camp in Bangkok. Our promoter called me with an opportunity to fight. It was Sunday evening when he called. He said the fight was scheduled for Wednesday evening. This was a fight at Ranger Stadium, and it was a big opportunity for me. Then he told me that I had to drop down to 147

pounds. At that moment I weighed 160 pounds, but I wanted the fight so much I told him I would do it.

I did not eat for 3 days. Each morning and evening I ran for miles, wearing a plastic suit that made me sweat. I cut my water intake, and beginning Monday night I had no water at all. I didn't even shower for fear that my skin would absorb moisture.

By Tuesday night I was massively dehydrated. My tongue was dry in my mouth. I could not sleep even 1 minute that night. Every second was torture. I daydreamed of water all night long. The morning finally came, and we went to the stadium for the weigh-in. I was 1/2 pound over the limit.

So I put on the plastic suit and ran. Then I went to a type of sauna and steamed. Still I was over the limit! I went for a second, a third, and a fourth run but could not get under the limit. By this time I was really getting sick. I went out for a final run. When I returned I took everything off and weighed for the fifth time. I made the weight, but I could barely stand.

My trainer insisted that I eat before drinking, but I could not swallow. I drank 4 liters of water and went to sleep. It seemed like only a minute later that they woke me to prepare for the fight. I was tired and very weak when I stepped into the ring that evening. I was nowhere near my best. I lost 17 pounds of water weight in 3 days, and I also lost a fight on points that I should have won easily. It was a big lesson for me.

Crash water-weight reduction is not as so common outside Thailand. It is not a particularly healthy practice, and I do not recommend it. In any event, a fighter is clearly at an advantage when he is near the top of whatever weight division in which he wishes to compete.

### Eating Strategically

What a person eats and drinks and how he does it are critical components of successful Muay Thai training. Villalobos avoids excesses and concentrates on maintaining a balanced and moderate diet at all times. He eats no meat other than fish and takes no supplements other than multiple vitamins.

Villalobos alters his diet as fight day nears. Approximately 2 months before a fight, Villalobos increases his intake of carbohydrates. Five weeks before the fight he cuts back on carbohydrates and increases his intake of proteins and vegetables, especially such green vegetables as broccoli and spinach. During the last week before the fight Villalobos drops virtually all carbohydrates. He eats moderately, emphasizing protein, vegetables, fruits, and juices. If he intends to cut his weight he will reduce his total calorie consumption considerably.

Villalobos recommends making the mid-day meal the biggest so that the body has access to energy and time to burn the calories. Prior to a workout it is wise to avoid eating or to eat only a small snack for energy about an hour beforehand. It is very important to eat after the workout. Eating 1 hour after a strenuous workout is optimal. It is at this time that the body needs nutrients to repair and build tissue.

It is important to listen to the body and not to overeat. Following are some dietary no-no's that fighters should avoid if they are serious about training and winning.

### Dietary No-No's

- Dehydration—drink a lot of water every day, but space it out so as not to drink too much at one time.
- Too much caffeine—some caffeine is fine, but too much will dehydrate the body.
- Alcohol—this dehydrates the body, as well as doing other things.
- Artificial stimulants—these take a great toll on the body and reduce strength rapidly.
- Drugs and tobacco—these shouldn't be used.
- Overeating—eat several small meals a day instead.
- Junk food and excessive sugar—these are empty calories that do little good nutritionally and must be burned up.
- Milk 1 hour before working out—this is the advice of the experienced fighters.
- Fried foods—these shouldn't be eaten.

### Meditation

Meditation is proven to have positive effects on the mind and body. Villalobos recommends meditation for Muay Thai fighters. He defines it as the process of sitting still and allowing the mind to relax. It is a part of his normal day of training. Following is a common Thai meditation that relaxes the body and helps the mind to become calm:

- Begin by sitting comfortably in a chair or cross-legged on the floor. It is important to keep the back straight.
- Place hands on your lap.
- Close your eyes and allow breathing to become calm.
- Focus concentration first on the face and will the muscles to relax in that area. Move progressively from one part of the body to the next, willing each to relax. Stop with the feet.
- Repeat the progressive relaxing sequence as many times as you wish. With each pass you will feel your body become more energized and more relaxed.

Meditation does not need to be mystical. Just sit still and let the mind go quiet and you will reap the rewards. Do not strain the breath. Sitting for long periods is okay, but beware of stiffness. Focus on a point in space, a soothing sound, or a positive idea. You can count slowly or create a pleasant mental image and let the mind drift into it. It is not necessary to try to eliminate all thoughts from the mind; just let the mind go quiet.

If you find meditation difficult, think back to childhood. Most people spent at least a short while during their childhood gazing at clouds. Recall how, after a minute or two, the clouds seemed to form recognizable shapes, such as animals, people, or buildings. This is an example of the mind relaxing and entering into a meditative state. Try to attain this level of attentive yet relaxed and receptive mindfulness when meditating. This is the right approach.

Active-mental-practice meditation is another highly productive method of meditation. Studies have proven that practicing physical skills mentally greatly improves performance in the real world. One famous mental practice meditation study was done with two groups of university students. Neither group had ever played basketball. Both groups were taught how to shoot free throws. Then the assessors recorded how many shots each student made. One group was required to practice in the gym each day. The other group was not allowed to practice but was directed to conduct daily mental practice meditation in which they visualized themselves shooting perfect free throws. At the end of the month, both groups were told to shoot free throws as the assessors kept track. The margin of improvement was statistically equal between the real-practice group and the active-mental-practice group.

Active-practice mediation can be done while sitting in a chair, sitting cross-legged, or lying down. Close your eyes and quietly visualize yourself performing specific Muay Thai techniques. You can expand this mental work to include visualization of an opponent or training partner. Repetition is the key to success in active mental practice meditation.

### Massage

Every fighter experiences fear and anxiety as a fight nears. The body is programmed to respond to fear with what is known as the fight-or-flight response. Inside the body the heart races and blood draws to the center of the body. Adrenaline kicks in, and the muscles tense. Peripheral vision is reduced, resulting in tunnel vision, and the higher functions of the brain are restricted as the primal brain takes control. To deal with this, Thai boxers follow a warm-up routine and ritual procedures. The prefight massage is part of this process.

Muay Thai prefight massage is a deep-tissue, full-body workover intended to prepare the boxer's body for the battle to come. Its purposes are a faster and more thorough warm-up and an avenue to help the fighter keep the fight-or-flight response in check.

The prefight massage presses blood into the muscles, thus providing warmth and oxygen. This gives the fighter full flexibility and makes it safer to kick and punch. The body that has been warmed by massage can react faster and better. Villalobos says that the prefight massages give him more awareness and more control over his body during a match.

"The massage helps me relax. It helps me to maintain a larger perspective on the fight," Villalobos says.

The prefight warm-up massage has benefits that last throughout the fight. Often fighters undergo a postfight massage as well. Liniment is often used to increase the effect. Villalobos says that postfight massages accelerate recovery.

It is important to apply the proper amount of pressure when performing a massage. The tendency of many is to apply too much pressure, thinking that more is better. Different fighters require more or less pressure, so the trainer must learn to accommodate the individual. The idea is to warm and relax the muscles. Following is a basic Muay Thai pre- and postfight massage routine.

### MUAY THAI PRE- AND POSTFIGHT MASSAGE

#### Face-Down Massage Sequence
- Ankles
- Calves
- Knees
- Quadriceps
- Buttocks
- Lower back
- Middle back
- Upper back
- Neck
- Biceps and triceps
- Forearms and hands

#### Face-Up Massage Sequence
- Feet
- Shins
- Knees
- Quadriceps
- Stomach
- Chest
- Head and temple
- Biceps and triceps
- Forearms and Hands

#### Sitting-Up Massage Sequence
- Shoulders
- Upper back
- Neck

The pre- and postfight massage should be deep but gentle. It is desirable to rub liniment into the muscles after the fight. Many fight trainers also do this before the fight.

Understanding Muay Thai strategy begins with a grasp of the key elements of fighter personalities. According to Villalobos there are four distinctly different types of fighters: (1) aggressive, (2) counter, (3) elusive, and (4) tricky. The next chapter explores these four types and provides strategies for responding to each.

# 5

# STRATEGIES OF THE FOUR TYPES OF FIGHTER

nderstanding the four primary types of fighter is the key to strategy in Muay Thai. The four types, as defined by Villalobos, are aggressive, counter, elusive, and tricky. The styles of the four types are intrinsic. Many fighters do not even know that they exhibit a readable fighting personality, yet all do.

The four fighter styles are universal to all martial arts, not just to Thai boxing. Different trainers may describe the four types with different adjectives, but they are clearly observable and basically the same for all. For example, well-known karate champion and promoter Karyn Turner identified the four styles as charger, blocker, runner, and elusive runner.

After fighting, coaching, and witnessing hundreds of matches, I am still convinced that there are only four main types of fighter in the karate world. As simple as it sounds, if you can beat these four fighters you can beat almost anybody in the world. Ninety-seven percent of all competitors use one of the four styles of fighting almost exclusively (Turner and Van Schuyver 1991, 67).

Once a fighter understands the four types he will never look at combat the same way. He will then be able to classify competitors and prepare strategies and cultivate techniques to take advantage of type preference and to overcome these "personality" differences.

## OVERVIEW OF THE FOUR TYPES

The strategy of the *aggressive fighter* is based on strength and raw power. This type is perhaps the easiest to diagnose because he continuously presses forward and attacks head-on. Bigger and more powerful fighters tend to favor the aggressive approach. Depending on

Four kinds of fighters: aggressive, elusive, counter, and tricky.

the fighter, this type can be very effective. Of the four types, however, the aggressive is the most primitive and most common.

Waiting is the hallmark of the *counter fighter*. Counter fighters rarely attack first. Their strategy is built around defensive positioning. They wait for the opponent to engage them and then respond. Their style is to dominate and crush the opponent with relentless attacks.

The *elusive fighter* moves all the time, forcing his opponent to avoid him and also to chase him. The elusive fighter evades punches and then strikes like lightning. He moves in and out of range constantly and very quickly. Speed and flexibility are the main tools of the elusive fighter. He often makes an opponent think that he is going one way then rushes in the opposite direction. Elusive fighters use lots of variations in timing.

The *tricky fighter* fakes more than any other type. Tricky fighters are sneaky; they are rule breakers. These guys live for the opportunity to knock an opponent out or damage him severely.

In effect, the sneaky fighter is a liar. His strategy is to deceive and trick his opponent. His goal is to win at any cost. Tricky fighters have a talent for drama and often use facial expressions and body language to intimidate the opposition.

In Thai boxing there is another basic element of complexity that fighters must contend with when constructing strategy. In addition to the four fighter personality types, there are four distinct ranges for fighting: kicking, punching, elbow/knee, and clinching. Only a very few fighters have real mastery of all four ranges. This rare person is called the *range-versatile fighter*. Such fighters are exceedingly dangerous.

A fighter's intrinsic type and his preference for range combine to form 16 distinct fighting styles (shown at the bottom of page 71). A fighter may, for example, face an aggressive kicker in one match and a counter kicker in another. You will also find tricky clinchers and elusive clinchers. There are elusive punchers, and there are aggressive punchers and so on.

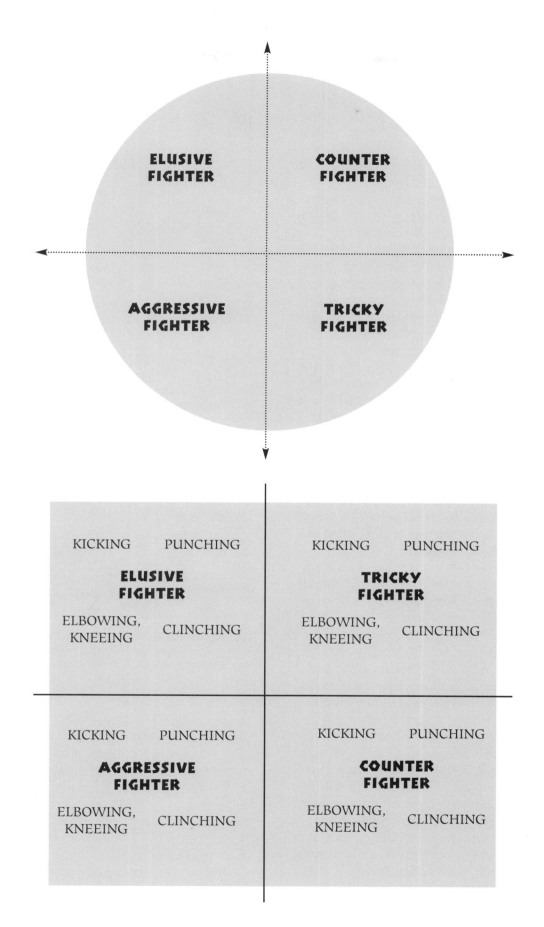

## THE AGGRESSIVE FIGHTER

*When torrential water tosses boulders, it is because of its momentum; when the strike of a hawk breaks the body of its prey, it is because of timing. Thus, the momentum of one skilled in war is overwhelming, and his attack precisely timed. His potential is that of a fully drawn crossbow; his timing, that of the release of the trigger.*
— Sun Tzu, *The Art of War*

The aggressive style is most natural for fighters who are big and very strong. This fighting type can be extremely effective especially when employed by a strong fighter. Aggressive fighters achieve quick success with their strength and drive. They usually don't employ a wide variety of techniques because they simply are not as important with this strategy. Aggressive types keep lots of pressure on the opponent. They are famous for explosive techniques. It is often the case that an aggressive fighter will defeat a "better fighter." That is to say, sheer power frequently defeats finesse, style, and clever technique.

It is common for an aggressive fighter to come straight at his opponent. The idea is to drive forward all the time until he knocks the other fighter out cold. As they are typically very strong fighters, the aggressive fighters can take a lot of hits. Think of Rocky, in the movie: lots of power, dogged determination, and a very high pain tolerance. Aggressive fighters don't use as many angles of attack as the other types do. As a rule they never back up, so footwork for this style is more limited than for the others.

Aggressive-style fighters typically have a lot of raw strength and power: their relentless, straight-ahead attacks leave their opponents with very little time to compose an attack of their own. In other words, the truly aggressive fighters force their opponents onto the defensive, pushing and pushing until the opponents are worn down.

There are some weaknesses to the aggressive approach to strategy in the Thai ring. Using so much energy in such an overwhelming manner takes its toll. Aggressive fighters often become run down in later rounds. If the aggressive fighter misses his objective of attaining a knockout or damaging the opponent severely in early rounds, he becomes susceptible to attack late.

Aggressive stylists are almost always less

Top: Aggressive fighter attacking with the elbow.
Above: Aggressive fighter attacks with the right knee, which Villalobos blocks with his knee.

strategic than the other types, and in many cases they are stronger but slower as well. Part of the aggressive fighter's game, as with every type, is psychological. If an aggressive fighter thinks he is stronger, then he automatically believes that he will win the match. This is the essence of the aggressive fighter's strategy. Therefore, never allow an aggressive fighter to think that he is stronger.

It is wise to avoid going head to head with an aggressive fighter early in the match. Doing so will

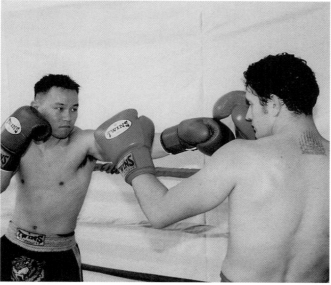

Top: An aggressive fighter attacks Villalobos with a high kick, which he evades by moving his upper body backward.
Above: This aggressive fighter attacks with a jab.

elusive style is the best to use against a purely aggressive opponent. Villalobos says an even better approach is a mixture of elusive and aggressive. The formula is to be more elusive in the early rounds and to become more aggressive as your opponent tires in the later rounds.

Early in his Muay Thai career Villalobos fought an aggressive fighter. Naturally aggressive himself, Villalobos went straight at him, employing what he now describes as "aggressive versus aggressive." His opponent was 172 pounds to Villalobos' 160. This is how it went:

My opponent was bigger, stronger, and younger. I went after him with everything I had. After the first round I was already tiring. He worked in the punching range a lot. I fought from the kicking and punching ranges. We both kept pushing forward at each other all the time. In the first round he hit me with solid cross. In the second round I got him with a cross. In the third round he was backing me up, and then I'd back him up. He hit me with his knee and knocked the wind out of me. I closed his eye with punches.

In the fourth and fifth rounds he was still hitting me with everything he had, and I was hitting him with everything I had. He could take a lot of punishment, and so could I. He never paced himself, and neither did I. We both went very hard all the way like a couple of pit bulls. Both of us took a beating, but in the end I lost the fight. I lost because he was stronger and I tried to fight aggressive to aggressive.

Nowadays I would never fight 100-percent aggressive against another aggressive opponent, especially if that fighter was stronger. Experience has taught me. Now my strategy with aggressive fighters is to be elusive and let them miss. I avoid their strength and shield and keep moving in and out. I hit and move. I move fast and stay elusive for at least one round to wear them down. Then, when they become tired I get aggressive and take them out.

allow him to see whether he is stronger or not and, if he is, to gain a psychological advantage. Avoid this by moving around a lot in the first round. Let him miss and hit him with hard counterstrikes. The goal is to frustrate him and let him wear himself out. Remember that, barring a knockout, Muay Thai matches go on for five long rounds.

It is smart to keep clear of an aggressive fighter for the first three rounds of a fight. This provides a much better chance of taking him down in rounds four and five. Theoretically, the

Although the best strategy against a purely aggressive fighter is to use an elusive style early and aggressive later, a counter fighter approach may also work. However, a counter strategist may get into trouble against an aggressive type because the latter constantly backs the counter fighter up and clogs his options. A tricky approach is generally less effective because the aggressive fighter will charge in, cutting out the time that the tricky fighter needs to set up his stratagems. Unless a fighter is significantly stronger than his opponent, the worst option is to go aggressive against an aggressive fighter because in almost all cases the stronger of the two will win.

### Aggressive-Style Fighting Strategies

Aggressive fighters are known for being more about the basic approach of relentless attack than for having well-planned strategies and tactics. It is possible, however, for a purely aggressive fighter to achieve greater results by applying some additional strategic thinking before entering the ring. Following are five strategies that work well for the aggressive type of fighter.

- Apply as much pressure as possible to "eat the other fighter's heart" and beat his spirit down.
- Shield or parry and attack right away.
- Advance with power and determination. Do not retreat.
- Apply strength to defeat technique.
- Strive for a knockout in the first round.

During the first weeks of his first trip to Thailand, Villalobos was given the opportunity to fight on the Thai island of Kohsamui. He accepted, and as it turned out it was a battle of two aggressive-style fighters bent on smashing each other at all costs. Here is the story in Villalobos' own words:

My promoter asked me if I wanted to fight. It was early in my training, but I felt ready and told him so. He said, "You have two weeks to prepare." He also told me that the fight would be held on the island of Kohsamui. My opponent was to be a middleweight Thai fighter from England. We heard that he was about my size and around 165 pounds.

Two weeks later we arrived at the stadium on Kohsamui. The guy was not a middleweight! When I saw the English guy I realized that the information we had was wrong. I could see that the guy was at least 180 pounds and stood at least 6 feet tall. At the stadium there were flags—one for Spain, my native country, and one for England. The crowd was really into it, chanting "Spain, Spain," or "England, England." The fight had been billed as a match between our countries.

He came at me fast in the first round. He was very aggressive and threw several powerful kicks. I blocked one of his round kicks, shielding [against] it with my leg. It was so powerful that for a minute I thought my shin was broken.

We went head to head for a long while. I saw that he was very strong and powerful but that his techniques were not clean. I threw a lot of aggressive foot jabs at him and moved to my left. He won the first round on points, but in the second round I got him in the clinch and nailed him with an elbow. I won the fight on a technical knockout. The crowd went wild chanting, "Spain! Spain! Spain!" Man, I can tell you there is nothing like that feeling. The English fighter went to the hospital and received seven stitches.

I won this fight because my techniques were better than my opponent's and because I held him in the clinch range where I had more skill. My style of fighting was the same as his, purely aggressive. If I were to fight with him again, I would alter my style and fight him with a combination of aggressive and counter styles.

### The Aggressive Fighter in the Four Ranges

An aggressive kicker will charge and attack relentlessly favoring low, middle, and high kicks all the while. To defeat him, fighters should use a mixture of counter and elusive fighting styles. It is important to stay out of the kicking range when fighting an aggressive kicker. Otherwise there will be a tit-for-tat power struggle, and the stronger fighter will win.

A good strategy for dealing with the aggressive kicker is to keep out of range and then suddenly move into very close range. In other words, alternate between being outside and then inside kicking range. Use knee and elbow and clinching counterattacks. Make elusive attacks in these ranges too.

If you happen to meet up with an aggressive-type fighter who is strong in the punching range and not very skilled in the other ranges, you have an opportunity to defeat him with counterkicking techniques. It is also wise to make use of elusive attacks against an aggressive puncher. These attacks must be carefully timed. Charge in and launch fast kneeing or clinching assaults.

Kicks take a lot more energy than punches. Strategy against an aggressive puncher is to use very close-range tactics and to avoid getting worn out too fast. Above all, stay out of boxing range when up against an aggressive puncher.

Handle an aggressive knee and elbow fighter by staying in the kicking and punching ranges. Work counter and elusive strategies against aggressive knee and elbow fighters. It is important to deny them access to their favorite range. Knee and elbow attacks are powerful but hard to lead with. Take advantage of speed and position and avoid being grabbed.

Understand that most fighters who are good with open knee and elbow techniques are also good at using them in the clinch. When up against an aggressive fighter, keep him from getting in close. Defense against neck grabs and sweeps must be maintained. Assume an elusive or counter fighter style.

If grabbed by an aggressive clincher, try to break the clinch right away. If it is not possible to escape the clinch, then press in as close as possible to eliminate the space that he needs to launch his aggressive clinch fighting techniques.

As stated previously, most fighters rely on one style of fighting and have a favorite range. Given all the strategic options, this may sound limited; theoretically it is. Such a fighter can be very effective, but just imagine how much more he would be if he increased his skill in the various ranges and also learned to adopt other fighting styles. In general, the more flexibility between style and range that a person has, the better shape he will be in when put to the test inside the ring.

## THE COUNTER FIGHTER

*The skillful warriors in ancient times first made themselves invincible and then awaited the enemy's moment of vulnerability.*
—Sun Tzu, *The Art of War*

The counter fighter is considered by many to be the most dangerous of the four types. Without a doubt, counter fighters are considered very dangerous animals. They are notoriously strategic in their approach to combat: they wait for opportunities and then strike with great accuracy. Counter fighters employ a defensive strategy but are not passive. Their method is to calculate everything. The counter fighter's pace is even, and his mind is always working. Counter fighters gauge distance and observe the angle of approach and techniques favored by their opponents. They are the chess masters of the ring.

Accuracy, timing, speed, and an almost scientific approach to fighting are the key strengths of counter fighters. Born strategists, they are naturally calm and analytical.

Counter fighters love to draw their opponents in. They move away from attacks with perfect timing: they parry, sideslip punches, evade with ease, and then strike hard before their opponents can recompose their guard. Counter fighters steal their opponent's strength while conserving their own.

As slick as they are, however, counter fighters do have a weakness or two. Since they are very calculating it is possible to confuse them by simply not giving them what they expect. Establishing a pattern and then abruptly breaking it can accomplish this. It is very difficult to counterattack effectively unless there is a pattern to predict. In other words, if they are not attacked in predictable ways, counter fighters cannot mount a reliable counterstrategy.

A combination of elusive, tricky, and aggressive fighting styles works best to defeat a pure counter fighter. Broken rhythms, fakes, and unpredictable attacks can mess up his game. Fakes make him waste energy and force him to recalculate. A stare into his eyes tells him, "I tricked you," and makes him worry. He can be controlled if he is made to react to the strategic use of elusive raids, tricky body language, and timed aggressive attacks.

Villalobos won the ISKA middleweight Muay Thai professional championship by knockout. His opponent was a skilled counter fighter from Russia, who was about 6 feet to Villalobos' 5 feet 9 inches. Villalobos defeated him by using a

Villalobos and his opponent in counter fighter stance.

combination of aggressive and counter fighter styling. Here in Villalobos' own words is how the fight went:

> The Russian was very tall and skinny. He was relatively weak in his upper body, and his legs were very strong. His boxing skills were excellent. In the first round he punched me many times. His accuracy was amazing. I tried to kick him and keep him in the kicking range, but his arms seemed to be longer than my legs! I fought him with an aggressive fighter styling but had a lot of trouble dealing with his punches and his counter-fighter styling.
>
> He continued to dominate the fight with punches through the second round. In the third round I began to mix aggressive styling with counter-fighter styling. I faked him and changed back and forth several times. This caused him to become more aggressive. He got out of his counter-fighter style. I took the opportunity to close the gap and get him in a clinch. From the clinch I was able to neutralize his punches and land some knee strikes. I won the third round.
>
> He came back hard in the fourth round and was really punishing me with punches. He got back into his effective

Top: When Villalobos attacks with a round right kick, his opponent counters with a left foot jab.
Above: Villalobos' opponent counters his cross with a knee.

> counterpunching game. Once again I pressed to clinch, but it was much harder to close on him this time. He would throw counterattacks with three or four very accurate punches and some kicks when we exchanged.
>
> I kept mixing aggressive with counter styling. Finally I threw a right foot jab that made him back into the ropes to evade. I rushed in and round kicked him to the ribs and then closed in to clinch. I held him

**FIGHTING STRATEGIES OF MUAY THAI**

tight and then opened to get space to throw a knee. Just then I heard shouting from my corner, "Pedro! Let him go!" I opened my arms and stepped back. He collapsed to the floor. Only my clinch and the ropes had been holding him up. His eyes were open, but even with the help of his corner guys he could not stand for at least 2 minutes. This guy was a very good fighter, and I believe that I won because I was able to alter from aggressive to counter style and also because I was able to force him into close-range situations.

Counter fighters are patient fighters. Going against them with a purely aggressive approach plays right into their hands. To beat a counter fighter you must become a little aggressive and a little elusive. It takes strategy to bring a counter fighter out of his defensive mode. To do so it is necessary to surprise and confuse him. Remember that good counter fighters are very accurate.

Another way to draw out a counter fighter is to fake weakness or an injury. It is important to confuse him. The counter fighter must not be allowed to measure his opponent's way of fighting. It is critical to mix ranges of attack and vary pacing between fast and slow, weak and strong, aggressive and passive. Cause the counter fighter to lose his counterattack accuracy by breaking his rhythm and confusing his plan. Keeping him from reading what is coming next is most important.

*If the defender has obtained an important advantage, then the defensive form has done its part, and under the protection of this success he must give back the blow, otherwise he exposes himself to certain destruction; common sense points out that iron should be struck while it is hot, that we should use the advantage gained to guard against a second attack.*
—General Carl Von Clausewitz, *On War*

### Counter-Style Fighting Strategies

When up against a skilled counter fighter you must be prepared to deal with him with great care. Remember, a counter fighter is the most analytical of all types. He will be studying everything you do and rapidly creating strategies to thwart anything you throw at him. The following five basic strategies work well against the counter fighter:

1. Let him miss and attack him on the way back.
2. Use speed to attack and to beat his counter.
3. Base everything on timing.
4. Relax and stay calm. Do not become overly aggressive.
5. Study and analyze the opponent to see what he has.

## THE ELUSIVE FIGHTER

*If I am able to determine the enemy's dispositions while, at the same time, I conceal my own, then I can concentrate my forces and his must be divided. And if I concentrate while he divides, I can use my entire strength to attack a fraction of his. Therefore, I will be numerically superior. Then, if I am able to use many to strike few at the selected point, those I deal with will fall into hopeless straits. The enemy must not know where I intend to give battle. For if he does not know where I intend to give battle, he must prepare in a great many places. And when he prepares in a great many places, those I have to fight in will be few. For if he prepares to the front, his rear will be weak, and if to the rear, his front will be fragile. If he strengthens his left, his right will be vulnerable, and if his right, there will be few troops on his left. And when he sends troops everywhere, he will be weak everywhere. Numerical weakness comes from having to guard against possible attacks; numerical strength from forcing the enemy to make these preparations against us.*
—Sun Tzu, *The Art of War*

Elusive fighters are extremely fast. Naturally elusive fighters tend to be less powerful than others in their weight bracket, so relying on an aggressive approach as a full-time strategy is not their best option. Early in their career the fighters of lighter build learn to take advantage of their speed and reflexes. They must rely on angles, mobility, and rapid footwork to defeat bigger and stronger opponents.

Elusive fighters seldom attack in straight lines. They fake a lot and may do so with head, hips, shoulders, arms, legs, and feet. Elusive fighters are masters of attack combinations, and their specialty is to get in, hit, and get out before getting caught.

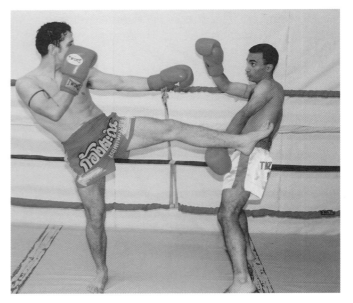

When attacked with a round middle kick, the elusive fighter (on the left) arches his body and lets the kick pass.

Elusive fighters are quick and very difficult to catch. Skilled elusives keep moving all the time. Elusive fighters, despite their constant movement, do not waste energy. They move to their own drum and maintain their own pace.

As do all the types, the elusive fighter has a weakness or two to exploit. The elusive fighter is typically not too strong, so it may be possible to take him out with far less effort than you would need with an aggressive- or a counter-style opponent. Remember almost all fighters have a natural type, and that type is a product of their own abilities. Elusives are elusive in part because typically they cannot take much punishment.

When going against an elusive fighter, begin with a mixture of counter- and elusive-style strategy. You should feign weakness and encourage him to be more and more aggressive. This strategy helps to settle the elusive fighter down and improve the odds of taking him out. Later in the fight you may choose to become more aggressive against the elusive fighter. Chasing him in the early rounds is a waste of energy. The general idea is to draw the elusive fighter into a trap and knock him out.

The biggest danger in fighting elusives is the fact that they are so hard to hit. They move like the wind, and it is difficult to gain leverage or positional advantage when fighting them. Elusives are masters at breaking their opponents' rhythm

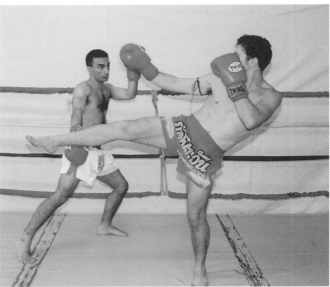

Here the elusive fighter (on the right) parries the foot jab to his left and then to his right.

and causing them to lose momentum. They take away their opponents' energy and disrupt their timing. Techniques and combinations that work well against aggressive and counter fighters may be useless on the elusive fighter.

Villalobos deliberately changed fighting styles from his natural aggressive to almost pure elusive recently when he confronted an accomplished counter fighter. Villalobos' strategy worked. He was able to confuse and then defeat his opponent. Here he recaps the fight:

The elusive fighter moves out of the way of Villalobos' kick.

## Elusive-Style Fighting Strategies

Elusive stylists are highly tactical fighters. They make use of their superior speed and misdirection to score. Following are five key strategies that the elusive fighter will likely deploy to take maximum advantage of the elusive style.

1. Speed
2. Surprise
3. Deceptive movement
4. Manipulation of the opponent to control his movements
5. Movement in all directions and angles
6. Mastery of footwork

## THE TRICKY FIGHTER

*All warfare is based on deception. Therefore, when capable of attacking, feign incapacity; when active in moving troops, feign inactivity. When near the enemy, make it seem that you are far away; when far away, make it seem that you are near. Hold out baits to lure the enemy. Strike the enemy when he is in disorder. Prepare against the enemy when he is secure at all points. Avoid the enemy for the time being when he is stronger. If your opponent is of choleric temper, try to irritate him. If he is arrogant, try to encourage his egotism. If the enemy troops are well prepared after reorganization, try to wear them down. If they are united, try to sow dissension among them. Attack the enemy where he is unprepared, and appear where you are not expected. These are the keys to victory for a strategist. It is not possible to formulate them in detail beforehand.*
—Sun Tzu, *The Art of War*

In the first round I tested this guy and saw right away that he was a defensive counter fighter. He would just wait for me to attack. When I did he would punch or kick really fast. I saw and felt that he had a lot of power, and I knew that he was just watching to see where I was open each time I came at him. When I stayed back, he would just wait. There was no way that he wanted to come after me. It was a good test for me because he was one of the most defensive fighters that I've seen.

I wanted to go after him aggressively, but I knew that I had to surprise and confuse him. I chose to fight him elusively. In the second round I deliberately attacked him using the same combination of jab, cross, and left round kick to the leg three times in a row. The next time I broke the pattern by faking first and then attacking with a foot jab, cross, round kick high combination. I continued to create and break aggressive patterns for the whole round. In round three I made him react to a bunch of different angles and fakes. By the fifth round I had him coming after me. I used an elusive strategy and got him out of his element. It was very close, but in the end I won this one on points.

Tricky fighters win by bending the rules and exploiting psychological weaknesses. Tricky fighters are deceptive and unpredictable opponents. The game they play is deliberately different from the one that their opponents play. Tricky types draw from an unlimited variety of head games tailored to suit each opponent.

Tricky-type fighters are also called dirty fighters because they will bend or break the rules to win. Tricky or dirty, however, does not imply out-of-control violence. For example, when Mike Tyson bit part of Evander Holyfield's ear off in a boxing match a few years back, this was not the work of a tricky-style fighter. What Tyson did was

Villalobos concentrates hard as he attacks the tricky fighter with a left leg.

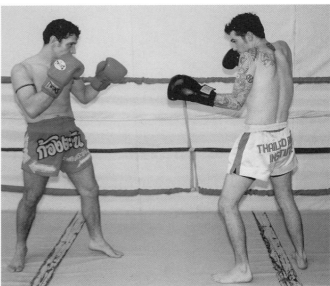

Top: The tricky fighter is trying to distract Villalobos.
Above: This tricky fighter exhibits an unorthodox stance.

nasty to be sure, but it was not part of a planned psychological strategy. Tyson's attack was aggressive to the extreme, but it cost him the fight and messed up his eligibility. Getting caught while breaking the rules is not a viable strategy.

Some say Tyson was enraged because Holyfield continually head-butted him during the infamous ear-biting match. Holyfield's can be classified tricky because he was not disqualified and it made his opponent freak out. He may have received warnings from the referee, but he broke the rules only marginally and perhaps for the specific purpose of discombobulating his opponent.

Mohammed Ali employed tricky fighter strategies all the time. He talked to his opponent's before, during, and after his fights, cajoling and attempting to psych them out at every turn. In the ring he fought with both an elusive and a tricky style. His mode of operation was to do the unexpected: tricky strategy was clearly a key part of his success. No one doubts the effectiveness of his mind games, and many since have emulated him.

In Muay Thai matches, tricky fighters often employ dirty tricks outside the referee's view. They might, for example, deliberately strike an illegal target such as the groin. In a clinch they might head-butt just enough to worry the opponent but not enough for disqualification. A

tricky fighter might stomp on an opponent's feet or break other rules specifically to confuse and disorient an opponent. Such strategies work best against less experienced fighters, and fighters who value and respect their opponents and honor the rules of the game are most susceptible to tricky strategies.

The tricky-type fighter's greatest strength is his unpredictability. You never know what a tricky fighter is going to do because his moves are strange and unpredictable. "Just when you think that you are figuring out his game he hits you with

The tricky fighter uses a strange movement before he attacks to trick Villalobos.

The tricky fighter fakes with his hand to distract Villalobos' attention. Then he attacks low when Villalobos looks at his hand.

some sneaky punch or kick," Villalobos says. The tricky fighter takes advantage of situations created by illusions. Tricky fighters seek to trick, disorient, and psych out their opponents and then hit them during the confusion.

The tricky fighter's greatest weakness is the possibility that his opponent will not react to the games and illusions. The tricky fighter is most susceptible to an aggressive-type fighter with experience and a cool head.

"To beat the tricky fighter you must show him that he is not upsetting you and that his tricks do not affect you," Villalobos says. "You demonstrate this by attacking him while he is doing his tricks. It is effective to aggressively plow into him while he is trying to do his tricky games."

When he starts to do something crazy, for example, immediately kick him. "Do not wait to see exactly what he is doing, just hit him hard," Villalobos advises. Take the opportunity to hit him during the time he is creating the illusion. "In this way, you take the power of illusion away from him."

You do not appear frantic or angry when striking the tricky fighter in the middle of his trick. The tricky fighter must be made to believe that his tricks are not working and have no effect.

Some additional examples of tactics used by tricky fighters include the tendency toward deceptive moves. For example, a tricky fighter might throw a jab at his opponent's face but deliberately aim it to the left of the head, creating the illusion that the jab is actually a hook. The trick is to cause the opponent to open his guard to provide space for a right cross.

Other examples of tricky techniques include upward jabs followed by low kicks and low kicks followed by punches to the face. A tricky fighter might fake the low kick to draw out a shin block and immediately follow the defender's leg back for a "half-kick" back in.

Tricky fighters like to use sounds to frighten or

disorient an opponent. Sometimes they'll act crazy or pretend to be tired or pretend to be strong when they are actually weak. Think of the tricky fighter as a masked opponent. Always his intention is to appear to be something other than what he really is in order to create and exploit an artificial advantage.

Villalobos and I witnessed a fight that was one of the participant's first amateur fights. It is a given that everyone who fights is going to be scared, especially in his first match. This man, however, was shaking like a rabbit. Moments before his fight he was obviously terrified and perhaps on the brink of breaking down.

Just before leaving the dressing room the novice fighter uttered, "Man, I don't know if I can do this. I don't have any experience. I don't know if I am ready for this." His trainer gave him a pep talk, and his friends slapped him on the back and encouraged him. He trembled all the way to the ring.

When he stepped through the ropes, his natural fighting style instantly emerged. Without hesitation he jumped into the air and stomped the ring. He shouted and whooped; then threw himself to his knees and pounded the floor with his palms. He carried on as his opponent and everyone in the audience looked on with shock.

When the bell rang the guy charged across the ring and threw himself at his opponent like a crazy man. Over and over he charged with seemingly reckless abandon. Several other witnesses queried later remarked that they were convinced he was drugged out. In fact he was totally drug free.

Right away the "crazy" guy had his opponent totally rattled. He landed a few blows and his opponent landed some, but it was clear that his opponent, like the audience, was freaked out. In the end, the "crazy guy" won easily against an opponent he should not have been able to defeat. His strategy was to psych out his opponent, making him think that he was either absolutely crazy or very high on PCP or some other powerful drug. The result of this strategy was victory for the tricky fighter.

## Tricky-Style Fighting Strategies

Tricky fighters are notorious for winning fights that they should not have been able to win. They use strategies to overcome power, technique, speed, and defensive finesse. Tricky fighters are sucker punchers and extraordinary gamesmen. When up against a tricky fighter, understand that he will use one or all of the following core strategies:

- Surprise
- Fakes
- Psychology
- All kind of tricks—some legal, some not
- Acting
- Language
- Odd or inappropriate facial expressions
- Rule bending
- Shocking and distracting behavior

## OVERVIEW OF THE UNIVERSAL FIGHTER

Even though every fighter has a natural and preferred fighting type, as discussed, a significant number of fighters can take on the attributes of one of the other types. Some fighters can flow between all four types. The person with mastery over all four types is called the *universal fighter*.

If a universal fighter also has the skill to fight effectively at all four ranges he is described as a *versatile-universal fighter*. The versatile-universal fighter is the most eclectic and perhaps the most dangerous opponent of all. Fighting him, if he exists, would be like fighting 16 different opponents at one time.

The universal fighter has a reason for moving from one fighting type to another. He does this strategically in order to adapt to the other fighter's style. It is a measure of skill to be able to change types, and it is a higher measure of skill to be able to change to the right type at the right time specifically to counter an opponent.

## Strategies of the Universal Fighter

*Consequently, the art of using troops is this: When ten to the enemy's one, surround him. When five times his strength, attack him. If double his strength, divide him. If equally matched, you may engage him with some good plan. If weaker numerically, be capable of withdrawing. And if in all respects unequal, be capable of eluding him, for a small force is but booty for one more powerful if it fights recklessly.*

—Sun Tzu, *The Art of War*

The universal fighter is the most formidable fighter of all. The truly universal Muay Thai fighter can fight in all four styles at all four ranges, thus making him something of a super fighter. Even more intimidating is the ability of the super fighter to adapt to strategies and change styles and range fluidly as needed in real time. In short, the universal fighter can become any type and is able to fight all the other fighters by applying the most appropriate style. He can bring the best style and range to any circumstance.

The universal fighter quickly determines where the other fighter is weak or strong and applies the appropriate strategy and tools to defeat him. The universal fighter is very adaptable and very flexible. Mentally he knows how to get where he needs to get without having a hard time. He is like a chameleon, able to change at will. Universal fighters are quite rare. They fight with less effort and greater effect than any other type. To become a universal fighter you must have natural talent, excellent coaching, and lots of experience in the ring.

Some trainers prefer to emphasize a fighter's natural type rather than attempt to teach him to achieve style adaptability. Developing a universal style requires massive amounts of work and is only possible with certain individuals. Having marginal skill in all areas does not qualify. In other words, being mediocre at everything does not make you a universal fighter.

Even the mighty universal fighter has a weakness. Discovering his weakness is much more difficult because the weak points will be well hidden in his versatile approach. Still, it is impossible for a universal fighter to be equally strong at every part of the game in every type and range. Somewhere in this set of possibilities a weakness lies.

How does a person take on a universal fighter? Become universal too. Like the kid's game of rock, paper, scissors, each style is superior to and inferior to another. Remember this formula:

Villalobos on the right during the Spanish championship fight in 1994.

aggressive over tricky, tricky and elusive over counter, elusive over elusive, elusive over aggressive, aggressive over all for the fighter who is stronger. When the universal fighter becomes aggressive, respond by becoming elusive. When the universal fighter gets tricky, respond by becoming aggressive. If the universal fighter converts to elusive, beat him with counter tactics. If the universal fighter moves into counter fighter mode, switch to the elusive style.

Versatile universal fighters are good at all styles and ranges, but each individual is better at some things than others. During the fight, observe which style and range the universal fighter seems best at and seek to exploit that weakness. When two universal fighters clash, the game becomes one of adaptability. The one with the greater experience and most adaptability will win this complicated game.

Above: Villalobos fighting in New York.

Right: Villalobos after a Muay Thai championship in Atlanta, Georgia.

## Universal Preference

*When I have won a victory I do not repeat my tactics but respond to circumstances in an infinite variety of ways.*

—Sun Tzu, *The Art of War*

Even the universal fighter has a natural type. This natural style is like a center of gravitation common to all fighters, even the most universal. The universal fighter's strongest type will almost certainly be his original and natural base. By studying his history you may be able to determine, before the match, which is his base type. This is helpful because his natural style is the area in which you are least likely to find a weakness to exploit.

Below Villalobos recounts a fight with a world-class universal fighter from Thailand:

I knew that this fighter was a champion in Thailand and that he was very good at all four ranges. He was a major champion with many, many victorious fights. I did not know until I got into the ring with him that he was a also a universal fighter.

My sense in the first round was that his type of fighting was counter style. His skill was very high, and I quickly realized that I could not win with him by being aggressive, my natural style. So I switched to elusive. I moved in and out but he quickly switched to elusive too, and his elusive skills were better than mine. I tried to switch to counter fighting, and he stayed elusive. He wore me down and then suddenly he turned aggressive and knocked me into the ropes. I got to my feet still playing defense, but it was no good. He stayed aggressive and attacked me in all four ranges. In the third he round knocked me out.

When I woke up I realized that I had faced not just a champion fighter but a real and truly universal fighter. I learned more from this fight than any fight in my career. This guy controlled me at every step. I couldn't do anything against him. From this fight I learned that to beat a universal fighter you must also be universal. This fight changed me forever. Now I train hard to be equally and highly skilled in all four styles.

The next chapter takes a look at what it takes to get ready for a match. This level of training is not for the faint of heart. It is a grueling process that only a few brave and hard-working souls have the depth for.

# 6

# BATTLE STRATEGY

*What is of supreme importance in war is to attack the enemy's strategy.*
—Sun Tzu, *The Art of War*

How does a fighter prepare for a match considering that there are so many fighting strategies available to each opponent? Villalobos recommends the following formula:

Villalobos and all four types of fighters: aggressive, elusive, counter, and tricky. As a universal fighter, Villalobos uses all four styles.

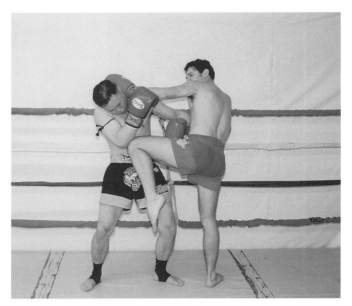

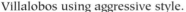
Villalobos using aggressive style.

1. Identify and understand your own fighting type and range preferences. Know your strengths and weaknesses.
2. Study your opponent's type, range preferences, strengths, and weaknesses.
3. Visualize your opponent and imagine that he is bigger, stronger, and faster, and has superior endurance.
4. Maintain faith in your own style.
5. Fight for the purpose of self-improvement.

This proven formula helps fighters maintain a positive attitude and gain psychological advantage. Attitude during the fight is critical to victory.

## KNOW THYSELF

*Therefore, I say: Know your enemy and know yourself; in a hundred battles, you will never be defeated. When you are ignorant of the enemy but know yourself, your chances of winning or losing are equal. If ignorant both of your enemy and of yourself, you are sure to be defeated in every battle.*
—Sun Tzu, *The Art of War*

To become a champion, you must identify and understand your own fighting type and range preferences. It is critical to know your strengths and weaknesses. It is important to recognize

Villalobos using elusive style.

## AGGRESSIVE FIGHTER

| Question | Circle One | |
|---|---|---|
| I attack first | 1 | never |
| | 2 | seldom |
| | 3 | sometimes |
| | 4 | mostly |
| I attack relentlessly | 1 | never |
| | 2 | seldom |
| | 3 | sometimes |
| | 4 | mostly |
| I rely on power to win | 1 | never |
| | 2 | seldom |
| | 3 | sometimes |
| | 4 | mostly |
| I push forward continuously | 1 | never |
| | 2 | seldom |
| | 3 | sometimes |
| | 4 | mostly |
| I hit first | 1 | never |
| | 2 | seldom |
| | 3 | sometimes |
| | 4 | mostly |
| I don't like to retreat | 1 | never |
| | 2 | seldom |
| | 3 | sometimes |
| | 4 | mostly |

SCORE: Add circled numbers _____

## ELUSIVE FIGHTER

| Question | Circle One | |
|---|---|---|
| I am faster than my opponents | 1 | never |
| | 2 | seldom |
| | 3 | sometimes |
| | 4 | mostly |
| I attack and retreat, moving in and out of range very quickly | 1 | never |
| | 2 | seldom |
| | 3 | sometimes |
| | 4 | mostly |
| My opponents are usually stronger | 1 | never |
| | 2 | seldom |
| | 3 | sometimes |
| | 4 | mostly |
| I rarely tire and seldom get hit | 1 | never |
| | 2 | seldom |
| | 3 | sometimes |
| | 4 | mostly |
| I use lots of combinations | 1 | never |
| | 2 | seldom |
| | 3 | sometimes |
| | 4 | mostly |
| I use lots of fakes | 1 | never |
| | 2 | seldom |
| | 3 | sometimes |
| | 4 | mostly |

SCORE: Add circled numbers _____

opportunities for personal development and victory as well as those that threaten to take it all away. In short, know yourself as a fighter and as a person.

A big part of knowing yourself as a fighter is being certain that you have identified your own fighting type. A fighter can determine his own fighting type by taking the following simple and straightforward assessment. After taking the assessment ask your training partners and trainer to confirm your accuracy.

## DETERMINE YOUR NATURAL FIGHTING STYLE

The accompanying chart is for determining a fighter's natural or base style.

Add your score for each type from the assessments above and place your numbers in the following grid.

**Aggressive**
   Your score: _____

**Elusive**
   Your score: _____

**Counter**
   Your score: _____

**Tricky**
   Your score: _____

Now look at the score. It may be obvious which style is more natural for you. If your score is extremely high in one area and low in the other three, the preference for that style is very high. There is nothing wrong with this as long as you also develop a high degree of adaptability. Any fighter can adapt to another fighter's styles by

## COUNTER FIGHTER

| Question | Circle One | |
|---|---|---|
| I almost never attack first | 1 | never |
| | 2 | seldom |
| | 3 | sometimes |
| | 4 | mostly |
| I shield or parry and counterstrike | 1 | never |
| | 2 | seldom |
| | 3 | sometimes |
| | 4 | mostly |
| I seldom advance, preferring to let my opponent come to me | 1 | never |
| | 2 | seldom |
| | 3 | sometimes |
| | 4 | mostly |
| I counterattack with combinations | 1 | never |
| | 2 | seldom |
| | 3 | sometimes |
| | 4 | mostly |
| I watch my opponent and plan my counterattacks to respond to his pattern of attack | 1 | never |
| | 2 | seldom |
| | 3 | sometimes |
| | 4 | mostly |
| I fight defensively | 1 | never |
| | 2 | seldom |
| | 3 | sometimes |
| | 4 | mostly |

SCORE: Add circled numbers _____

## TRICKY FIGHTER

| Question | Circle One | |
|---|---|---|
| I like to win at all costs | 1 | never |
| | 2 | seldom |
| | 3 | sometimes |
| | 4 | mostly |
| I break the rules of the game | 1 | never |
| | 2 | seldom |
| | 3 | sometimes |
| | 4 | mostly |
| I play mind games with my opponents | 1 | never |
| | 2 | seldom |
| | 3 | sometimes |
| | 4 | mostly |
| I try to psych my opponent out and hit him while he is off guard | 1 | never |
| | 2 | seldom |
| | 3 | sometimes |
| | 4 | mostly |
| I look for ways to cheat | 1 | never |
| | 2 | seldom |
| | 3 | sometimes |
| | 4 | mostly |
| I talk and or use body language to intimidate my opponents | 1 | never |
| | 2 | seldom |
| | 3 | sometimes |
| | 4 | mostly |

SCORE: Add circled numbers _____

increasing his skills in the different types or developing a response strategy to the various types. For example, if you are an aggressive fighter with no inclination to learn to fight in the other modes, you can still adapt by devising strategies that help to accommodate the other styles.

Some fighters are very high in two types. These fighters are flexible between two styles and can flow between them at will. A small number will find that they are high in three types, and a still smaller number will be about equal in all four.

"If you are high in all four types your versatility and natural adaptability are very great, and you are, or are on your way to becoming, a universal fighter," Villalobos says.

## RANGE STRATEGY

Since Thai boxers compete in four different

ranges, the game they play is very complex. By understanding that some ranges can be used to counter others is critical to good strategy.

There are no pat answers, but in general it is wise to counter kicking with kicking. This is especially effective in the first round when both fighters are fresh. Kicks take a lot of energy, however, so it is wise change strategies in later rounds and begin a process of tactical countering using kicks with punches.

Knee and elbow attacks can be neutralized with a counter strategy favoring pushing the opponent away and striking with kicks and with punches. It is vital to move and to stay out of the knee and elbow range when faced with a skilled fighter of this preference.

Use the following grid as a general rule for countering the four ranges, but remember that Muay Thai fighting is a game of deception and

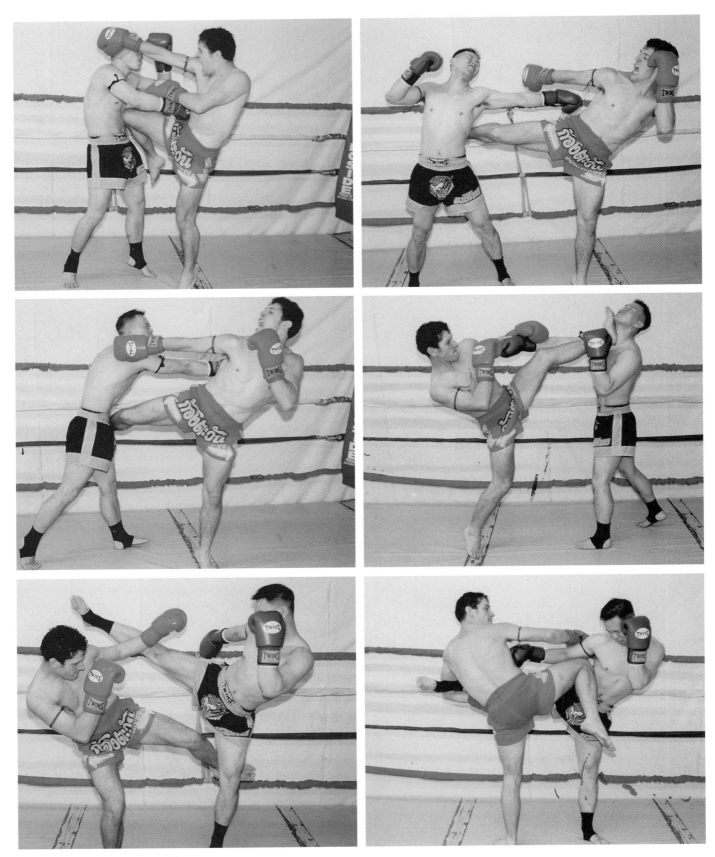

Villalobos using counter style.

**FIGHTING STRATEGIES OF MUAY THAI**

Villalobos using tricky style.

## KICKING-RANGE ASSESSMENT

| Question | | Circle One |
|---|---|---|
| I am most comfortable fighting in the kicking range | 1<br>2<br>3<br>4 | never<br>seldom<br>sometimes<br>mostly |
| Long-range kicks are my most reliable weapon | 1<br>2<br>3<br>4 | never<br>seldom<br>sometimes<br>mostly |
| Long-range kicks are my most accurate weapon | 1<br>2<br>3<br>4 | never<br>seldom<br>sometimes<br>mostly |
| Long-range kicks are my most effective weapon | 1<br>2<br>3<br>4 | never<br>seldom<br>sometimes<br>mostly |
| Long-range kicks are my fastest weapon | 1<br>2<br>3<br>4 | never<br>seldom<br>sometimes<br>mostly |
| I can defend myself best in the kicking range | 1<br>2<br>3<br>4 | never<br>seldom<br>sometimes<br>mostly |

KICKING SCORE: Add circled numbers _____

## PUNCHING-RANGE ASSESSMENT

| Question | | Circle One |
|---|---|---|
| I am most comfortable fighting in the punching range | 1<br>2<br>3<br>4 | never<br>seldom<br>sometimes<br>mostly |
| Punches are most reliable weapon | 1<br>2<br>3<br>4 | never<br>seldom<br>sometimes<br>mostly |
| Punches are my most accurate weapon | 1<br>2<br>3<br>4 | never<br>seldom<br>sometimes<br>mostly |
| Punches are my most effective weapon | 1<br>2<br>3<br>4 | never<br>seldom<br>sometimes<br>mostly |
| Punches are my fastest weapon | 1<br>2<br>3<br>4 | never<br>seldom<br>sometimes<br>mostly |
| I can defend myself best in the punching range | 1<br>2<br>3<br>4 | never<br>seldom<br>sometimes<br>mostly |

PUNCHING SCORE: Add circled numbers _____

complex strategy. Understand that these general guidelines are a starting point from which to build a strategy, and remember that every opponent is different and that no single strategy will work against all comers.

## Assess Your Range Strategy

### Kicking Range
- Counter kicking with kicking in early rounds
- Counter kicking with boxing later in the fight

### Knee and Elbow Range
- Counter with pushing and kicking or boxing
- Counter kneeing with kneeing

### Punching Range
- Counter punching with kicking
- Counter punching with punching
- Counter punching with knee strikes

### Clinch Range
- Counter clinching with inside clinching and attack with knees and throws
- Counter clinching with outside clinching and attack with punches, elbows, and knees

## Assess Your Range Preference

Muay Thai fighters operate with fantastic flexibility because of the number of body weapons allowed and because four different fighting ranges are legal and effective. Thai boxers train in all of the ranges; however, almost everyone has one range in which he is most comfortable and effective. Use the following assessment to determine your range preference and identify your range strengths and weaknesses.

Take a look at the range assessment scores. It is most common for a fighter to have a preferred

## KNEE/ELBOW-RANGE ASSESSMENT

| Question | Circle One | |
|---|---|---|
| I am most comfortable fighting in the knee/elbow range | 1<br>2<br>3<br>4 | never<br>seldom<br>sometimes<br>mostly |
| Knees and elbows are my most reliable weapons | 1<br>2<br>3<br>4 | never<br>seldom<br>sometimes<br>mostly |
| Knees and elbows are my most accurate weapons | 1<br>2<br>3<br>4 | never<br>seldom<br>sometimes<br>mostly |
| Knees and elbows are my most effective weapon | 1<br>2<br>3<br>4 | never<br>seldom<br>sometimes<br>mostly |
| Knees and elbows are my fastest weapon | 1<br>2<br>3<br>4 | never<br>seldom<br>sometimes<br>mostly |
| I can defend myself best in the knee/elbow range | 1<br>2<br>3<br>4 | never<br>seldom<br>sometimes<br>mostly |

KNEE/ELBOW SCORE: Add circled numbers _____

## CLINCH-RANGE ASSESSMENT

| Question | Circle One | |
|---|---|---|
| I am most comfortable fighting in the clinch range | 1<br>2<br>3<br>4 | never<br>seldom<br>sometimes<br>mostly |
| Attacks from the clinch are my most reliable weapons | 1<br>2<br>3<br>4 | never<br>seldom<br>sometimes<br>mostly |
| Attacks from the clinch are my most accurate weapons | 1<br>2<br>3<br>4 | never<br>seldom<br>sometimes<br>mostly |
| Attacks from the clinch are my most effective weapons | 1<br>2<br>3<br>4 | never<br>seldom<br>sometimes<br>mostly |
| Attacks from the clinch are my fastest weapons | 1<br>2<br>3<br>4 | never<br>seldom<br>sometimes<br>mostly |
| I can defend myself best in the clinch range | 1<br>2<br>3<br>4 | never<br>seldom<br>sometimes<br>mostly |

CLINCH SCORE: Add circled numbers _____

range. Some fighters are very comfortable in two or more ranges. A small minority of fighters are equally effective in all four ranges. The greater the skill in all four ranges, the higher the adaptability to various opponent strategies.

## DETERMINING UNIVERSALITY

Recall that the definition of a universal Thai fighter is one who is highly skilled and equally proficient in all four types of fighting (aggressive, elusive, counter, and tricky) and equally proficient at all four ranges (kicking, punching, knee/elbow, and clinch).

Use the chart above to rate yourself against the universal model.

To create a personal development chart use the template on the following page. The goal for students of the art is to develop skills in all

areas. Periodically retake the assessments for fighting type and range and rechart the scores. The idea is to identify and purge holes in the fighter's game. In other words, this is a tool to facilitate training with the goal of becoming a universal fighter.

## KNOW YOUR OPPONENT

Before the fight it is valuable to research an opponent's type, range preferences, strengths, and weaknesses. Ask questions of others who have fought this opponent. If there are videos of this particular fighter try to obtain and study them. If possible, go and see him fight. Will it be an even match or a repeat of David versus Goliath? A fighter can use the following diagnostic tool to determine how he stacks up against a particular opponent.

| UNIVERSAL FIGHTER | | YOU | | UNIVERSAL FIGHTER | | YOU | |
|---|---|---|---|---|---|---|---|
| Elusive: | 24 | Elusive: | ____ | Elusive: | 24 | Elusive: | ____ |
| Kicking: | 24 | Kicking: | ____ | Kicking: | 24 | Kicking: | ____ |
| Punching: | 24 | Punching: | ____ | Punching: | 24 | Punching: | ____ |
| Knee/Elbow: | 24 | Knee/Elbow: | ____ | Knee/Elbow: | 24 | Knee/Elbow: | ____ |
| Clinch: | 24 | Clinch: | ____ | Clinch: | 24 | Clinch: | ____ |
| TOTAL: | 120 | TOTAL: | ____ | TOTAL: | 120 | TOTAL: | ____ |
| UNIVERSAL FIGHTER | | YOU | | UNIVERSAL FIGHTER | | YOU | |
| Elusive: | 24 | Elusive: | ____ | Elusive: | 24 | Elusive: | ____ |
| Kicking: | 24 | Kicking: | ____ | Kicking: | 24 | Kicking: | ____ |
| Punching: | 24 | Punching: | ____ | Punching: | 24 | Punching: | ____ |
| Knee/Elbow: | 24 | Knee/Elbow: | ____ | Knee/Elbow: | 24 | Knee/Elbow: | ____ |
| Clinch: | 24 | Clinch: | ____ | Clinch: | 24 | Clinch: | ____ |
| TOTAL: | 120 | TOTAL: | ____ | TOTAL: | 120 | TOTAL: | ____ |

## PERSONAL DEVELOPMENT CHART
### Add your scores in each box.

| | |
|---|---|
| Kicking Score____    Punching Score____<br><br>**ELUSIVE FIGHTER SCORE**<br><br>Elbowing, Kneeing Score____    Clinching Score____ | Kicking Score____    Punching Score____<br><br>**COUNTER FIGHTER SCORE**<br><br>Elbowing, Kneeing Score____    Clinching Score____ |
| Kicking Score____    Punching Score____<br><br>**AGGRESSIVE FIGHTER SCORE**<br><br>Elbowing, Kneeing Score____    Clinching Score____ | Kicking Score____    Punching Score____<br><br>**TRICKY FIGHTER SCORE**<br><br>Elbowing, Kneeing Score____    Clinching Score____ |

## SELF VS. OPPONENT DIAGNOSTIC TOOL

| You: Score 0 or 1 | | Your Opponent: Score 0 or 1 | |
|---|---|---|---|
| Skilled in aggressive style | | Skilled in aggressive style | |
| Skilled in counter style | | Skilled in counter style | |
| Skilled in elusive style | | Skilled in elusive style | |
| Skilled in tricky style | | Skilled in tricky style | |
| Skilled in kicking range | | Skilled in kicking range | |
| Skilled in punching range | | Skilled in punching range | |
| Skilled in kneeing/elbowing range | | Skilled in kneeing/elbowing range | |
| Skilled in clinching range | | Skilled in clinching range | |
| More experienced than this opponent | | More experienced than you | |
| More knockouts than this opponent | | More knockouts than you | |
| Fight record much superior to this opponent | | Fight record much superior to yours | |
| Your trainer's record much superior to this opponent's trainer's record | | Your opponent's trainer's record much superior to your trainer's record | |
| Faster than this opponent | | Faster than you | |
| Stronger than this opponent | | Stronger than you | |
| Better conditioned than this opponent | | Better conditioned than you | |
| Trained 1 or more years longer than this opponent | | Trained 1 or more years longer than you | |
| Trained full-time to prepare for this fight | | Trained full-time to prepare for this fight | |
| Fighting for your home crowd | | Fighting for your opponent's home crowd | |
| You have more heart | | Opponent has more heart than you | |
| More limber than this opponent | | More limber than you | |
| **SCORES** | | | |

A fighter has an excellent chance to win if his total score is 50 percent higher than his opponent's. If it is 50 percent lower than the opponent's, the odds are he will lose badly. If a fighter's score is equal to his opponent's the odds are 50-50 regarding who will win. Fighters should diagnose themselves and their opponents to obtain a comparison. Without this evaluation it is anybody's guess who will likely be victorious. More important, it is difficult to formulate a meaningful strategy without this basic information.

From this diagnosis, fighters can gain information by which to orient their training for the purpose of maximizing their odds of winning a particular fight. If an opponent's total score is considerably higher, you can still win by using a strategy that takes advantage of your strengths while exposing the weaknesses of an opponent. For example, an opponent might be an aggressive-type fighter who is very strong in general and really good in the clinch, and has a superior fight record. Strategic preparation for this situation should include training to enhance both elusive and counter fighting skills. A fighter should also work hard on his clinch game to survive close encounters.

It is apparent from the diagnostic tool and from the above example that the advantage goes to the person with the most points, but victory can go to the one with the best strategy. Surely David's score would have been very low in contrast to Goliath's. Yet David's strategy was superior, and his victory was absolute. Any fighter can do the same if he aims his "sling" at the opponent's weakest component.

Part of preparing for a fight is strategic thinking and planning, as in the above illustrations. Another important aspect of preparation is improving technique and technical skill, as shown throughout this book. Equally important is mental preparation. Fighters commonly refer to the mental part of the fight as "eating the opponent's heart." Winning is more than beating someone physically; it is just as much about dominating him psychologically.

To prepare for the psychological part of the fight, Villalobos recommends visualizing the opponent as someone much larger and more dangerous than he actually is. To get ready for a fight Villalobos visualizes the worst possible scenario. In his mind, he sees the opponent as strong, bigger, faster, and

more technical than he is. Then, in the real fight, if the opponent has a weakness—and all opponents do—it is a pleasant surprise and an uplift to the heart when it is revealed.

Visualizing the opponent as bigger than life makes you train harder and be stronger in the face of challenge. It gives a person a psychological advantage and a better chance to "eat the opponent's heart."

Self-defense is an important part of the Muay Thai fight game. Fighters must know that they are truly ready before putting themselves in the ring. They must be capable of defending against injury. Make no mistake, Muay Thai boxing is a rough sport, and the possibility of serious injury or even death is very real. Knees, ankles, backs, shins, legs, necks, and ribs are vulnerable in Muay Thai. Just about every bone in the body is at risk of fracture. There have been matches in which even femurs were broken. A fighter can reduce the likelihood of injury by making certain that he is absolutely prepared mentally, physically, and psychologically before stepping into the ring.

## CULTIVATING UNIQUE TACTICS

Every fight and every fighter are unique. Strategy is made in advance of the fight, and tactics are applied on the inside of the ring. Tactics must be flexible and highly adaptable. It is possible to end up in a battle with an opponent who fights differently than research indicated. In every case you must expect the unexpected and be prepared to alter tactics. Keeping a bag full of unique techniques and tactics to be employed in difficult situations can make the difference between success and failure.

Muay Thai fighters evaluate their opponents during the first round of any fight. It is wise to save energy and test the opponent and learn as much about him as possible during that round. Strategy for the rest of the fight must be adjusted based on what is learned in these critical first 3 minutes. Following are common tactical considerations:

- If you're tired, do not let the opponent know.
- Appear tough at all times no matter how what.
- Keep your eyes open and look straight at the opponent.
- Never show weakness.

- Never expose your back.
- If the opponent lands a hit, do not show that it hurts.
- Study the opponent all the time.
- Look into your opponent's eyes with a face that lets the opponent know that he is going to be hit hard.
- Smile if you are hit by the opponent.
- If your opponent smiles, smile back.
- Keep your mouth shut.
- Trick his mind; eat his heart.
- Make him think he cannot win.
- Mix up the pace.
- Mix up the ranges.
- Stay relaxed except when striking.
- Mix unorthodox techniques with orthodox techniques in unpredictable combinations.
- Fake injury or weakness to gain advantage.
- Conserve energy until late in the fight.
- Cause the opponent to waste energy.

Create a customized bag of tricks and use them to win. Remember that at least half of any battle is psychological. No matter what happens, always keep faith in yourself. On the television series *Star Trek*, Captain Kirk once said that there are two kinds of people: those who believe in themselves and those who don't. These paraphrased words are the absolute truth. Belief in self is fundamental for victory for Thai boxers and for every other competition worth pursing.

Fighters must develop and hone their skills and then trust in themselves. "Believe in yourself and always fight for noble reasons," Villalobos says. "Remember that the point of competition is to get better at what you do. Winning is great, but the real victory is self-improvement. If you win but learn nothing in the process, then you gain nothing. If you lose but gain valuable knowledge about yourself and your fight game, then you actually win more. Of course, it is glorious to win and learn."

The next chapter explores the battle tactics of Muay Thai boxing. Remember, strategy is what one does before the fight; tactics are the application of technique during the battle.

# 7

# BATTLE TACTICS

nce the techniques are clean and the strategies are in place, you must be concerned with the tactical side of fighting. At the core are a series of defining principles. First among these are the methods of defending oneself against any strike. Next are the elements of timing that are factored into all defensive actions. Then there are four possible modalities of attack. Finally, there are several key rules for positioning yourself within the ring.

Villalobos steps with his right leg onto Trammell's left knee and then grabs behind his head with the left hand.

Trammell parries Villalobos' foot jab.

Villalobos takes Trammell's kick with his body.

Once the tactical principles of Muay Thai boxing are understood, you are ready to formulate specific tactics for each of the four ranges.

### MODES OF DEFENSE

The first mode of defense in known as *interception*. If an opponent can be beaten to the punch or kick it is possible to intercept his power. The experienced fighter, for example, may perceive that his opponent is about to throw a punch. Moving at lightning speed, he sends a foot jab into the opponent's middle just before the puncher commits himself. Thus the punch is intercepted and neutralized.

The second mode of defense is *shielding*. Shielding works, but there is a price to pay because the blocker must absorb all of the attacker's power on the defending limb. In Muay Thai, there is a very real possibility that the shielding limb will break under the blow. Still, shielding is an important element of defense and often the only option available.

The third mode of defense is *deflection*. Imagine a punch coming at a fighter's head. Say that it is a right cross. The fighter moves slightly to the left and taps the incoming punch with his left glove. The tap causes the punch to change direction and miss. This is accomplished without the defender's having to absorb the power of the

attack. Deflection leaves the defender in a strong and balanced state ready to counterattack.

The fourth mode of defense is called *evasion*. Imagine that a fighter throws a foot jab at an opponent and that the opponent moves to the side. The attacking foot hits nothing but air. The fighter fires off a follow-up round kick to the opponent's torso. The opponent moves again, and the attacker hits nothing. Each time the attacker misses the defender, the defender gains excellent advantage for counterattack and the attacker struggles to regain position.

The final mode of defense is called *trapping*. For example, a Thai fighter may evade or shield himself against an incoming kick and then grab the leg. Once the leg is grabbed, the opponent can be swept or attacked in a number of ways.

Aggressive fighters try to intercept or beat their opponents to the punch. Counter fighters are skilled at shielding and deflection. Elusive fighters specialize in deflection and, especially, evasion. Tricky fighters are unpredictable, often choosing the defensive mode that is most unexpected. All Thai fighters are trained in trapping and may use this skill to defeat a variety of different attacks.

### ELEMENTS OF TIMING

To fully understand the elements of defense

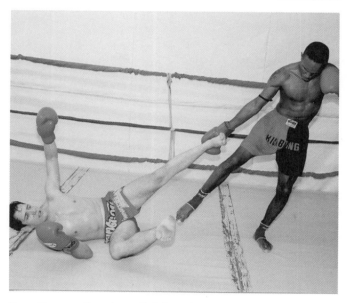

Top: Villalobos steps and kicks low behind Trammell's knee.
Above: Trammell does a cut-kick.

Top: Trammell grabs Villalobos' left middle kick and cut kicks his supporting leg.
Above: Trammell grabs Villalobos' left kick and cut kicks his supporting leg, bringing him down.

and the elements of attack you must know about the three elements of timing: *before*, *during*, and *after*. Consider these examples. Fighter A throws a cross at fighter B. If fighter B intercepts fighter A's attack by beating him to the punch he is applying element number one, *before*. Basically any attack that is prevented by any preattack is being thwarted by the timing principle of acting "before" the other acts.

The second element, *during*, refers to any

action that takes place while another action is taking place. For example, if one fighter parries another fighter's punch, he is acting during. If a fighter deflects another's punch, he is also acting during.

The third principle, *after*, is any technique that follows another. If, for example, a fighter kicks and his opponent evades the counterattacks, he is acting after.

Everything that happens in the action of a

Trammell moves back as Villalobos attacks with a round kick.

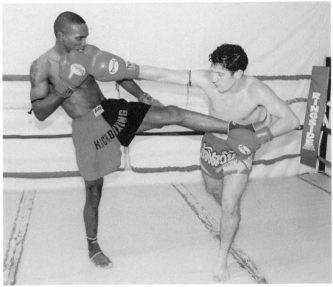

Top: Here Villalobos grabs Trammell's foot jab and counters with a cut-sweep kick on his supporting leg. Above: Grabbing Trammell's foot jab, Villalobos is now ready to execute a cut kick.

fight happens within the bounds of these three principles of timing. Nothing else is possible. Knowing this and building a strategy around this are critical to success as a fighter.

## MODES OF ATTACK

The four modes of attack are deceptive, intervention, simultaneous, and avoid and attack.

A *deceptive* attack is any attack preceded by a feint or some other element of deception. Elusive fighters are particularly adept at employing deceptive attacks.

An *intervention* attack is one that happens before the opponent is able to launch his own attack. Aggressive fighters excel at these preemptive attacks. Another key mode of attack is known as the first-strike phenomenon. Street fighters call this the sucker punch. If an attacker is able to strike without telegraphing his intention, he has first-strike advantage. For example, if an attacker throws a punch, the defender must perceive that the punch is being thrown and then respond. Response time is not sufficient to block or avoid a fast-moving punch. Remember driver's education? It takes up to 2 seconds for the average driver to perceive and respond when the driver in the vehicle ahead hits his brakes.

A Muay Thai fighter can certainly respond more quickly than the average driver, but the defender is at a tremendous disadvantage from a fast-moving first strike. Try the following exercise to get a better understanding of this.

- Player A holds both hands out in front. Player B stands with his hands to his side. Player B attempts to slap the back of either of Player A's hands at will. Even though Player A knows that the strike is coming and where it will be

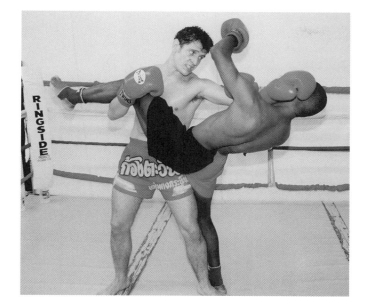

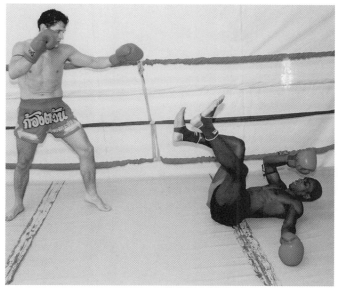

Here Villalobos' grabs Trammell's left knee from underneath and pushes him away with this left arm so that Trammell loses his balance and falls to the ground.

Top: Villalobos' steps up on Trammell's left leg and comes down with a right elbow.
Above: As Trammell attempts a left-knee circle, Villalobos stops it with a right front knee.

coming from, he will still find it difficult to move his hands away before Player B slaps them. If Player A is quick and skilled at not telegraphing his movements, Player B has very little chance of beating him.

• The next mode of attack, *simultaneous*, happens at the same time you shield from, deflect, or evade an opponent's attack. For example, imagine that a fighter throws a right

cross. You parry with your left and simultaneously punch with your right. It happens at the same time, that is the key.

• The last mode of attack, the *avoid and attack*, is any attack that follows an opponent's attack. If an opponent throws a round kick and you evade it and then counter with your own kick, this is an example of avoid and attack.

Trammell attacks with a left middle round kick. Villalobos counters with a spinning back elbow to his face.

## REASONS FOR ATTACKING

An attack is typically attempted for one of three reasons: damaging, disrupting, or confusing the opponent.

Attacks meant to damage the opponent are power shots that might do enough damage to earn a knockout. This might be a head blow or a body or leg blow, depending on the situation. It could be an attack meant to obtain a full or a technical knockout. Either way it is intended to end the fight, to hurt the opponent.

A disruptive attack is not intended to do significant damage. Its purpose is to harass, tire, or gain points on the opponent, or to set him up for a knockout attack later in the game. Jabs are commonly used as disruptive attacks. Some attacks are designed to confuse the opponent, as in the example of a tricky-style shot to a nonlegal target.

The next mode of attacking relies on the dual skill of hitting an opponent where he is standing and predicting where an opponent might move to when the attack occurs. If the opponent stands in one place, you can simply attack him in that space. If he is moving about, you must attack where he will be when your weapon arrives. If the opponent moves, hitting him while he is in motion is similar to duck hunting. Hunters aim just slightly ahead of the flying duck to allow for the speed of the bird in relation to the speed of the shot.

Top: Trammell uses his right knee to attack.
Above: As Trammell attacks with a round kick, Villalobos moves back to let the kick pass.

Finally, there are targets more worthy of attack than others. Striking them requires the skill of precision striking. The head, neck, torso, hips, and thighs are common Muay Thai targets. Muay Thai fighters quickly learn which targets are easiest to hit and which cause the most damage.

## RULES OF THE RING

Muay Thai fighters in Thailand follow a code

Trammell absorbs Villalobos' round kick to the body.

Top: Villalobos anticipates Trammell's move and attacks with a right knee.
Above: Trammell attempts a left knee, which Villalobos fends off with a right elbow down to Trammell's leg.

of conduct for the ring. These rules are partly for culture and partly for combat. From the cultural perspective, Thai fighters always bow before entering and leaving the ring. Thai boxers enter the ring by climbing over the ropes, never going through them. Going under or through the ropes demonstrates disrespect for the head. Maintaining respect for the head by keeping it above the ropes comes from the Buddhist tradition. In fact, the head is held above pretty

much everything in general. Villalobos points out that only the monkon can go on the head. It is a great insult, for example, to point or hold your feet above another person's head.

There is another serious taboo in Muay Thai: women are not allowed inside a man's Muay Thai ring. Their presence is considered extremely unlucky. This tradition may never change given the deeply held cultural paradigms of Muay Thai. There are, however, women's Muay Thai rings in modern-day Thailand, so who knows what may happen one day?

Ring flooring is made of a variety of materials. Some of the materials are slick, and some are not. It is wise to experiment with the flooring upon entering the ring. With some types of flooring, it is possible to gain traction by putting a bit of water on the feet. Generally speaking, canvas mats are the best.

The fighter who controls the center of the ring typically controls the fight. Right-handed Thai fighters, therefore, strive to keep their left foot in the center of the ring as much as possible.

It is important to stay away from the ropes. When in the middle of the ring, a fighter can move in four directions and use all his body weapons. Fighters must have mobility in all four directions in order to attack and defend successfully. If a fighter's back is against the ropes, he is in trouble because he can only move in three directions. It is

Villalobos steps on Trammell's left knee and attacks with a left knee to the face.

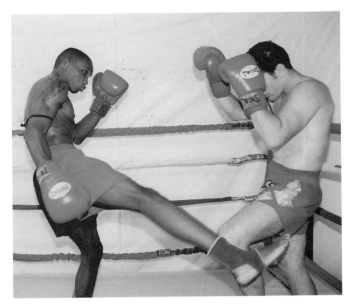

Villalobos uses his left knee to block Trammell's low kick.

even more important for a fighter to stay out of a corner. If a fighter is cornered, he loses three directions and most of his body weapons. The only way out is through the opponent.

When a Muay Thai fighter gets pushed against the ropes he will probably spring off the ropes and counterattack. If a fighter pushes an opponent into the ropes, he must expect such a counter. Experienced fighters gain power from the spring of the ropes and may deliver very strong counterstrikes as they fly forward. Being on the ropes is always a disadvantage because the odds are with the fighter who stands free of the ropes.

Sometimes Muay Thai fighters clinch, and both end up against the ropes. This is a dangerous moment for both. When this happens to a fighter, he must take great care not to be thrown or to fall over the ropes and out of the ring. Muay Thai ring ropes are lower than Western boxing ropes, so falling out is a distinct possibility and a real danger to the fighters.

Thai fighters try to force each other into the corners because getting out of the corner is very difficult. The rules for the corner are simple: (1) stay out of it, and (2) try to put the other guy into it. When a fighter gets caught in the corner, the best way out is to try to turn the opponent and push him into the corner, thus reversing the situation. This can be accomplished by clinching with and twisting the opponent.

Thai fighters gain points when they knock or sweep an opponent to the floor. If a fighter stumbles from an attack and his glove touches the floor, it is considered a knockdown. If he is swept from his feet or thrown, he loses one point. If a fighter slips he must jump back to his feet very quickly or he may lose a point.

From any fall or stumble it is important for fighters to return to their feet immediately. Fighters who take their time getting up signal that they are tired. Fighters do not want the judges or their opponent to make that assumption.

## RANGE TACTICS

As the reader has seen, there are four ranges for fighting in Muay Thai. These are kicking, boxing, knee-and-elbow, and clinch range. Every fighter, except for the universal fighter, has one or two ranges in which he is better and others in which he is weaker. Likewise, each opponent has similar strengths and weaknesses in his fight game. "Tactics rely heavily on making your opponent play your game while avoiding playing your opponent's game," Villalobos says.

The game of tactical distancing in modern-day Thai boxing is similar to an Old World duel with a couple of weapons of choice, such as pistols or swords. The Old World duelist who won the draw chose the weapons. Of course, he picked the

From the plam, Villalobos turns sideways and moves out of the way so that Trammell loses his balance and falls to the ground.

weapon that he was best with and, if possible, avoided the one that his opponent was particularly skilled with.

Fortunately, in a Muay Thai match fighters always get to "choose their weapons." Fighters choose to fight at the ranges in which they are most competent and avoid the ranges in which their opponents excel. The fighters choose to compete in kicking, punching, knee-and-elbow, or clinch range or some combination of the four.

But what about fighters who are new to Muay Thai and have not developed a particularly strong tactical game in any of the four ranges? New fighters will do well to determine which range they have the greatest aptitude for and develop skill in that area first. It is important to remember that some ranges are harder to master than others.

### Kicking Range

Kicking-range tactics work well for fighters with lots of stamina and flexibility. Remember, it takes a lot more energy to kick that to use the arms for striking.

### Kicking Range

Punching range takes a lot less energy to work from than the kicking range, but you must be able to get inside the opponent's long kick range.

### Knee-and-Elbow Range

Knee-and-elbow range requires an even higher degree of skill in closing the gap.

### Clinch Range

The clinch range is extremely effective yet quite difficult. There is a complex science of tactical fighting at this range. From this closest of all ranges fighters can sweep and also throw elbows, knees, and kicks. Clinch range is by far the hardest to master. It is the most secretive part of Muay Thai and perhaps the most difficult for Western students to gain access to.

At this moment in Muay Thai history, the Thais have mastery of the *plam lam* (clinch) and

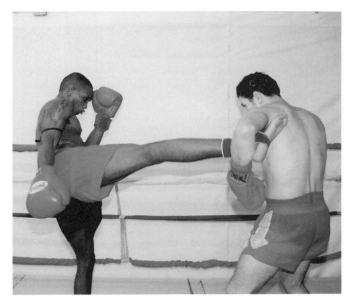

The four ranges (clockwise from top left): kicking, punching, elbowing, and clinching.

seem somewhat reluctant to share it with the outside world. Perhaps this is an element of the art that some hold back to maintain a level of supremacy over non-Thai practitioners. Or maybe it is simply the most advanced and difficult of the Muay Thai skills, and thus few Westerners have been able to train in Thailand for the time needed to gain real mastery of it. Regardless, the clinch is a major part of the game and a really important aspect to master.

The clinch, according to Villalobos, is "all about body motion and footwork." When one fighter grabs another his body must be straight.

The grabbing hands should be formed like a cup with one on top of the other behind the opponent's neck. Toes face to the outside, with the heels off the ground and the knees slightly bent. When a Muay Thai fighter grabs his opponent's neck he does not pull down with his arms. The goal is to get the other fighter to bend forward by hanging onto his neck like a monkey. In this way, a fighter uses his body weight rather than just arm strength to bring his opponent down.

When in the clinch Muay Thai boxers keep their chins down. They do not allow any space between their opponents and themselves. If they

**FIGHTING STRATEGIES OF MUAY THAI**

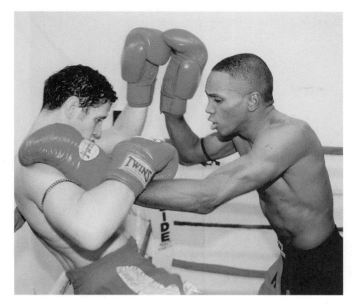

These photos demonstrate action in the punching range.

do allow space they will immediately receive a knee or elbow strike. A fighter must stay as tight against the opponent as possible and only allow space when it is time to throw a technique. The space should be closed immediately when the attack is done to avoid counterattacks.

If a fighter does not wish to attack with an elbow he must create space from inside the clinch. This is done by opening a bit of space in the upper part of the clinch. A fighter must push the opponent away to gain space to throw a knee strike. Whenever fighters push to create the space needed to attack from the clinch, they must do so

very quickly. It is critical not to press down with the arms during the struggle because it wastes energy. Thai fighters always clinch using their body weight.

The best target to strike from the clinch is the opponent's head. For example, a knee to the head may be enough to score a technical knockout. Every fighter knows this, of course, and will try to resist and counter by pulling his opponent's head down using body weight. Both fighters resist being toppled in the clinch by keeping their bodies straight and their heads high.

When clinching, a Muay Thai boxer grabs an opponent's head with both hands for maximum leverage. A fighter cannot bring an opponent's head down by grabbing at the nap of the neck. Most fighters grab at the top of the back of their opponents' head, pressing their elbows into the clavicle area to gain leverage. This grip gives fighters leverage from three points of pressure: at the back of the head and on either side on the clavicles. Thus skilled Muay Thai fighters have tremendous leverage and a real advantage in the clinch. Once in this position, fighters add body weight and pull other fighters over and into a knockout knee attack.

There are many variations of the clinch position, and each variation has its advantages and disadvantages. In a full clinch, the dominant fighter has his arms on the inside and enjoys maximum leverage and control. The fighter who has his arms on the outside in a full clinch hold is in a position of disadvantage and minimal leverage.

It is difficult in the clinch to get into a good position from which to strike.

In the clinch, fighters use body weight more than arm strength to bring their opponents down.

The plam, or clinch, is the most advanced of the Muay Thai skills and the most difficult to master.

Villalobos keeps his chin down and keeps as close to his opponent as possible in the clinch until he is ready to throw a right circle knee.

In a half-clinch situation, a fighter's right hand goes over the top of the other fighter's head and the elbow is pressed against the other's clavicle. In this position, the second fighter also has one hand on the other's head and one elbow on the other's clavicle. This is a mirror position and affords no advantage to either fighter.

In another form of clinching one fighter grabs the other in a bear hug. This is a body clinch in which one fighter's arms reach around the other's body. From this position, the fighter who holds is able to throw knees while maintaining control. The full-body clinch can be done from several different angles.

There are at least a dozen possible clinch positions and transitional clinch positions, each providing opportunities for attack or defense. In general, when in any sort of clinch, the closer you

This would be a good opportunity for Trammell to throw a right to Villalobos' face.

After pushing to create space from inside the clinch, Villalobos launches a right knee attack.

Keeping the body and head straight prevents a fighter from being toppled while in the clinch.

are to an opponent, the safer you are.

Each of the four ranges has its tactical advantages and disadvantages. Clinch range is, by far, the most complex and difficult to master. However, it is also, the most versatile range for those skilled in its use.

# 8

# THE MUAY THAI JOURNEY

n ancient times Asian cultures struggled for survival, for land, and for power. Before firearms, weapons were limited and battles were fought at very close range. Hand-to-hand combat was common. The metal, the wealth, and the skill needed to create weapons of high quality were scarce. Wars were common, and soldiers tended to get killed quickly. Replacements were expensive to arm and train. From this primal struggle and over countless generations, Asian battle techniques were formed and perfected. The original martial arts were actually war arts made up of deadly battlefield killing methods and techniques.

Over the centuries the ancient war skills were ritualized to an amazing degree. In many Asian societies the warrior knowledge and techniques evolved into disciplines of mind, body, and spirit with the potential to do more than just kill. Thus the ancient battlefield techniques became the personal arts of war and ultimately martial arts. Over time the martial arts became more civilized, deeply spiritualized, and informally codified.

Muay Thai is one such art with a rich and ancient history. Thai boxing, as a ring art, was established in the early decades of the 20th century. But Muay Thai as a martial art evolved from the empty-hand component of the ancient, venerable, and unbelievably deadly martial art known today as krabi-krabong, the ancient war art of Thailand that is still practiced today as a martial art rich with ritual and filled with deeply spiritual content.

Blood on a spear or sword and survival in battle were not enough for the ancient war masters. They understood that only by harnessing the power of martial technique and seeking the spiritual path would they achieve personal growth and self-knowledge. There

is, to put it another way, no soul in fighting without principle or purpose. The ancient krabi-krabong practitioners came to realize this and became something more than battlefield killers. They became martial artists in the full sense of the term. They blazed the way for countless others to follow.

Today the people of Thailand are not regularly called upon to use their hand-to-hand martial arts skills on the battlefield. The skills and wisdom of the ancient ways live on in the Muay Thai camps and in krabi-krabong training halls across the country. The art lives on because those who practice it and teach it remember the history and honor the spirit of the ancients.

Muay Thai matches began in ancient times. Often these competitions were held on special occasions. Victorious boxers were sometimes given positions of importance in the military. From ancient times until now ritual and ceremony have defined Muay Thai and linked it to the rich culture from which it hails.

The spiritual aspect of Muay Thai is at least as important to the fighters and to some fans as the actual contest. Every aspect of the art is steeped in spiritual tradition and ancient culture. Perhaps the most important ritual seen in Muay Thai training is the wai kru and the ram muay. (Wai kru means respect for the teacher, and ram muay means boxing dance.) Wai kru is sometimes used to mean both the respect gestures and the boxing dance.

Every Muay Thai fighter performs the wai kru ritual before every fight. The ritual performed before each fight is actually part of a larger set designed to demonstrate respect among student, teacher, family, community, king, and God.

At each phase of training, fighters participate in these various stages of the kru rituals:

- *Keun kru* (also called *yok kru*). This is a ritual of acceptance to training, and it is performed before an image of Buddha, typically on a Thursday. This ritual happens after an apprenticeship period and at a time when the instructor is ready to formally accept the student and the student accepts the instructor and agrees to follow the rules. The student promises loyalty to the teacher during this ritual.
- *Kronb kru*. The kronb kru ceremony happens upon the completion of a fighter's training and at a point when the fighter is able to compete at a high level and also competent to instruct others in the art.
- *We wai kru*. This is the annual ceremony dedicated to teachers in which students renew their promise of loyalty and respect.
- *Wai kru*. This ritual is performed by each fighter before every competition to show respect to the fighter's teacher and teacher's teacher. It also expresses respect for the king, the person overseeing the matches, and to God. The wai kru also serves to focus the fighter's concentration and loosen muscles before fighting.

The keun kru acceptance to training ceremony is especially important because it symbolizes the bond between mentor and disciple and sets the stage for all levels of the wai kru tradition. The newly accepted student repeats the following oath (Kraitus and Kraitus 1988, 29):

1. I will look after myself so that I am clean, strong, and behave with honesty.
2. I will not bully the weaker. We will love one another, be united, and help one another whenever possible.
3. I will make good deeds beneficial to the others and be loyal to the nation.
4. I will avoid any cause of disorder.

Kraitus and Kraitus also write that "there is an old saying that anyone who has not behaved in accordance with the oath shall be doomed." Suffice it to say that the Muay Thai community takes the oath of the keun kru very seriously.

## RITUAL ON FIGHT NIGHT

Ceremony and ritual are part of every aspect of training and every part of competition. Thai matches are alive with music that is also rich with symbolism. The music of Muay Thai is called *sarama*. At the big stadiums in Thailand live bands play the music. The instruments used in the sarama are the *ta pong* or *glon-kag* (two-face drum), *toe pee java* (Javanese flute), and the *ching* (cymbals). Music is important to the wai kru ritual and a tangible part of the fight itself. Sometimes fighters move in time to the music. The spectators thrive on it, and indeed it has a major effect on the atmosphere of the contest.

Fighters perform the wai kru and ram muay rituals while the music plays. The lively and compelling music continues throughout the entire fight. During the actual match, you can see the fighters keeping a rhythm during some parts of the match. In fact, one of the purposes of the music is to drive and inspire the pace of the fight. For example, observers will hear tones that drive the fighters along and then high tones meant to pump up the pace of the fight. The fighters are lifted and motivated by the rising and lowering of the music. The ritual music is part of the culture of Thailand, but the most important things are the rhythm and the audible encouragement of the fighters to go harder and harder.

On fight nights, the fighters prepare for their matches by performing the rituals of respect. The first part of the ritual sequence is the wai kru, which is performed in honor of teachers, parents, and ancestors. The second ritual, the ram muay, is to demonstrate respect for the spirits of Muay Thai. The wai kru and ram muay rituals consist of six major parts:

1. Fighters conduct the ritual "sealing of the ring." Fighters walk the ring sliding their glove along the ropes as they go and paying respect at the corners.
2. Fighters perform the first part of the ram muay, kneeling on the mat.

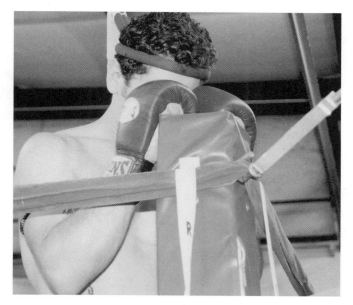

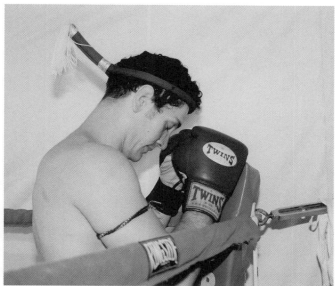

Ceremonial sealing of the ring before the fight.

3. Fighters perform the second part of the ram muay, standing.
4. Fighters pay respect to their opponents.
5. Fighters remove the mongkon.
6. Fighters bow to their teachers.

Each match lasts for five rounds. The rounds are 3 minutes each. Breaks between rounds last for 2 minutes. A referee follows the fight inside the ring. Two judges watch from just outside the ring. A fight can be won by points and by knockout. (Under some rules three knockdowns in the first round terminate the match.)

Muay Thai is extremely popular in Thailand. People go to stadiums or watch it on television. There are fights at the major stadiums in Bangkok almost every day and many more at smaller stadiums around the country.

Each Thai camp has its own version of the wai kru and ram muay. A Thai camp's wai kru is its signature: it can be thought of as a sort of brand or living symbol of the school. The dances of various camps are recognizable to the people in the stands. Just by watching the ritual fans know exactly where the fighters come from.

The motions of the wai kru and ram muay are

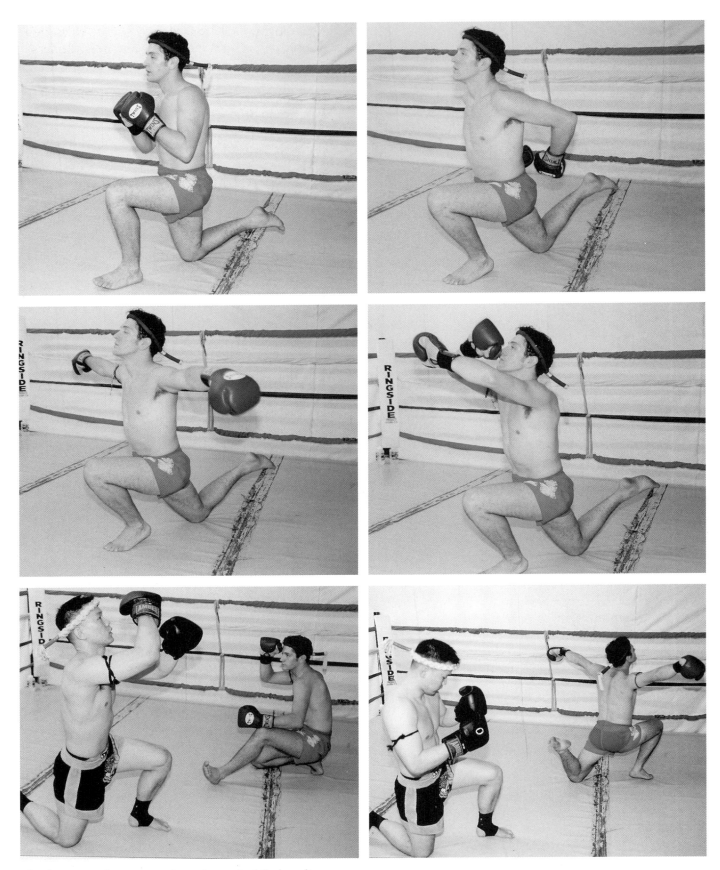

The first part of ram muay is performed while kneeling.

**FIGHTING STRATEGIES OF MUAY THAI**

highly stylized and beautiful to behold. Actions in the dances are symbolic of such things as a hunter's quest, animals in motion, and birds in flight. While each school has its own version, there are commonalties between all. In general there are two parts of the ram muay: the first part is from the ground, and the second part is done standing up.

The wai kru rituals are similar to the rituals of krabi-krabong. It is estimated that the wai kru tradition is many hundreds of years old, having its origins on the ancient battlefields of Siam. In those days, soldiers gave thanks and drew on powers to protect them from sword and spear.

Thai fighters in the United States may or may not participate in the customary rituals. (Some Western fighters and trainers believe that the rituals add no value.) Villalobos disagrees: he believes that performing the rituals is essential to retaining the integrity of the art.

Villalobos argues that without the rituals Thai boxing will cease to be a culturally significant activity. It is ritual that separates Thai boxing from raw fighting. It is ritual that links Muay Thai to its rich heritage and honor—and that maintains its civilized character. The rituals and culture are what make Muay Thai more than just a ring art; they make it a true and venerable martial art as well.

It is certainly true that the people of Thailand hold teachers in high respect. Instructors are respected at a level second only to family and God. It is considered the duty of the student to demonstrate respectful behavior and to work hard to achieve the instructor's goals.

Thai boxers believe that they will be rewarded for the proper treatment of their teachers. Boxers expect to benefit by:

1. bringing honor to their school and family,
2. becoming prosperous,
3. teaching others, and
4. advancing the Muay Thai art.

## SPIRIT OF THE WAI KRU

The ancient Thai warriors lived in a culture with strong spiritual belief. The supernatural powers were considered to play a big part in a warrior's success in battle. Prayer before battle included a call to the supernatural forces to enter the warrior's body and fill him with invincibility and power.

Different powers were thought to emanate from connection to and favor with specific gods of war, including Pra-Lai Penk, Hanuman, Kun Pan, Oran Pet, and Kong-Kah Derd (Kraitus and Kraitus 1988). It is from this warrior tradition that the wai kru of today evolved. Thus the wai kru is not to be taken lightly. To the Thai people wai kru is a deeply spiritual and important ceremony steeped in mystery and symbolism.

In part the modern-day wai kru is a tribute to the gods, and for many Thais this means Pra Isuan, the creator of the universe (Kraitus and Kraitus 1988). Through the music and the ritual, fighters open themselves to the presence of the holy spirits and the powers that may emanate from the divine. Through the ritual, boxers seek to tap their spiritual self and the powers of the supernatural. If successful, they enter a realm of existence without time or physical limitations, becoming what might be described as channels for supernatural forces.

Many boxers chant religious verses known as *kah-tah* during the rituals to evoke the supernatural powers. These spiritual verses are chanted silently, and as the fighter repeats the words in his mind he thinks of holy powers and may seek to visualize God. Thai boxers try to allow their soul to leave their body to be replaced by a holy spirit. The result is a fighter whose entire mind, body, and spirit are altered to achieve the highest potential in battle.

The wai kru ritual and the Muay Thai matches themselves are a deeply spiritual

The second part of ram muay is done standing.

endeavor for all participants. In Thailand, fighting without seeking the altered state of spiritual connectivity would still be fighting, but it would not be Muay Thai. Muay Thai is therefore much more that a boxing technique. To the Thais, Muay Thai is a spiritual practice.

There is great honor in being a Muay Thai boxer. It is expected by the people, the practitioners, and the trainers that the skilled Muay Thai fighter be a gentleman at all times. To be anything less is to dishonor the culture, one's family, teacher, community of boxers, and God. The following comment by Panya Kraitus and Dr.

Pitisuk Kraitus speaks eloquently of the Thai code of honor and to the spirit of the Wai Kru:

Any boxer who is too proud of himself and likes to quarrel and fight with others outside the ring is not in any way a brave man or a capable boxer, but a bully whose mind is filled with hatred and anger. A real boxer will never bully or intimidate anyone. Even when he is provoked, he should restrain himself from retaliating for fear of damaging his reputation.

The real boxer will be brave when

bravery is required, such as fighting for his homeland and even sacrificing his life. Such action would strengthen not only his own honor and reputation but also those of his family. The real boxer should aim to create unity, make himself useful to the society, be a good patriot, and avoid unruly behavior.

Common to all wai kru rituals is a procedure known as the "three steps of the boxer." In this ritual, the fighters go to the four sides of the ring representing the four geographical directions and demonstrating respect for religion, country, parents, and teacher.

### The Wai Kru Feeling

Some Muay Thai fighters report a feeling of near-euphoria when performing the wai kru before a fight. Perhaps this feeling is derived from the mixture of adrenaline and focused control. Villalobos says he conducts a "concentrated self-dialogue," during the ritual. He shuts out the noise of the crowd and turns his mind inward in intense concentration.

"I become quiet inside and listen to myself. I am very aware of the environment, and I take in the energy. I feel profound respect for my teachers and for the art. My fear and nervousness diminish, and I go into a place where I don't care what happens—a place of power but most of all a place where I know that doing my best, not just winning, is what is truly important," Villalobos says.

Some fighters perform their wai kru dance exactly the same way every time. Villalobos varies his wai kru performances slightly:

I don't do it exactly the same each time. I mix some different dance elements depending on what I feel in the moment. This it is my way of becoming connected to the environment. If you do the wai kru the exact same way every time you may become like a machine and lose attention. Doing the wai kru with creative variety keeps me fresh and focused.

It takes a couple of months to learn the basics of the wai kru, but it takes lots of practice to do the wai kru well. Fighters spend their careers refining and perfecting their personal wai kru dances.

## TRAINING IN THAILAND

### The Country

It is best if you have a friend from Thailand to sponsor and guide you through the process of locating a camp for training. It is possible, however, to do this alone. The Internet is a good place to look for camp recommendations. When you arrive in Thailand, the Tourist Authority of Thailand is a good place to begin searching for camps that offer Muay Thai training.

All you really need to pack for training in the camps are Thai shorts, bag gloves, and hand wraps. Other than that you need only bring money for training, a positive and humble attitude, and a sincere desire to work hard and learn well.

It is wise to take a basic course in the Thai language before traveling to Thailand in search of training. Understand that the Thai people are very friendly to people they perceive as respectful. The Thais do not respond well to loud and boisterous behavior. They appreciate and honor humility and like it when people are delicate in manner and in speech.

Thailand is very different from any Western country. The Thai people are very open and good-natured, but they will treat foreigners badly if the latter behave in an ugly manner.

It is important to always act respectfully and to show it. Thai people demonstrate respect with their behavior and with the traditional Thai bow. "To do the bow, simply place both of your hands together in front of your face, smile, and bow slightly," Villalobos says.

It is perfectly acceptable for foreigners to perform this courtesy. The bowing gesture is something similar to shaking hands in the West, and it is expected. The Thai people respond favorably to it.

The Thai people are extremely clean. It is important, therefore, to dress well and stay clean at all times. Villalobos recalls taking many showers every day during his trips to Thailand. "Thai people appreciate a person who has both a warm heart and a clean body," he says.

Most Thais are Buddhist, and some behavior is considered enormously offensive to the faithful. Chief among these taboos is the pointing of the feet.

"Never point your feet at a Thai person. Do

not place your feet upon a table or high up on a chair. If you hang pictures on the wall, do not have someone's head under someone else's feet. To do so is a serious insult to people of the Buddhist faith," Villalobos says.

Buddhists believe that the head is important and that it should be above the lower parts of the body. To touch someone on the head, even a child, is considered an insult. "Always be respectful of the people and of their traditions and their religion and you will find yourself showered with respect given in turn," Villalobos says.

(Bargaining is expected in Thailand. The price of almost everything on the street, including *tuk-tuk* rides, entertainment, and books is open to negotiation. Store prices, however, are usually fixed.)

"It is never a good idea to brag about your strength or your record as a fighter or your experiences in the ring. Adopt a more selfless and humble mode and know that the Thai people will warm to you quickly if you respect them and show it in this way," Villalobos says.

It is always a good idea to purchase a couple of maps before setting off: one for Bangkok and one for Thailand. It is easy to find a hotel and possible to stay very cheaply if you shop a bit. It is a good idea to use tuk-tuks to get around in the city. It is fairly easy to get around and to get established in a Muay Thai training camp even without a local friend or sponsor.

**Choosing a Muay Thai Camp**

It is beneficial to visit a number of Thai camps before making a decision. It is a good idea to build extra time into travel plans for the search-and-evaluation process. For example, you can learn a lot by spending an entire day at each camp just as an observer.

A small number, perhaps 5 percent, of all of the Bangkok camps have English-speaking trainers: most of them speak English for the fun of it. Be advised, however, that a few of these trainers are speaking English for a reason: to expand their profits by capturing the overseas market.

Villalobos recommends not limiting yourself to English-speaking trainers. Most learning happens in the following steps: (1) observe, (2) do, (3) receive feedback, and (4) do again. Body language is far more important to the communication of the art than words.

"If you go to a non-English-speaking trainer you will learn just fine, and as a side benefit you will pick up more of the Thai language," says Villalobos.

Begin by visiting Thai boxing stadiums. Villalobos recommends going to the "Muay Thai shop" inside each stadium. Once there, politely inquire about which camps in the area have the best fighters. You can learn a great deal about the local camps in this manner. When you have finished your homework, begin visiting camps on the list in a systematic way. Start by introducing yourself and politely asking permission to observe the day's training.

If things look good, consider investing in a single day of training. At the time of this writing, the cost for one day would be somewhere between 200 and 500 Thai baht (at a rate of U.S.$1 to 35 or 40 baht). You should not expect to learn a great deal of new material in this single day. Trainers will not invest much time and energy in a foreigner until they are sure of their character. Think of it as a "get-to-know-you day." Observe the way the trainers handle the students. Watch how the fighters do their techniques and take note of the flow and the intensity of their training. Check out the conditioning of the boxers and be sensitive to the mood of the place. Pay careful attention to the heavy-bag and Thai-pad workouts. Listen to the tone of voice used by the trainers. Watch for red flags such as lack of discipline, sloppy technique, and trainers or promoters who lose their temper.

Make the decision to stay or move on more on the basis of the way the trainers work with the regular students. If everything looks good, commit to a week or more and give the trainer a shot. The more time that you commit, the more likely the trainer is to open up.

By watching, you can learn how the fighters execute their techniques and observe the pattern and intensity of their training. It is important to watch the bag work and pad work. Observe the conditioning of the boxers. If their conditioning is very high, chances are the training is good.

Villalobos says, "Keep your spirits high and your mind and heart open at all times during your search. With time, perseverance, and a humble attitude you will find excellent training, and you will be accepted graciously by both the students and the trainers."

Bangkok is the hub of Muay Thai competition in Thailand. There are many stadiums in the city, and the level and quality of the fights is very high. Because of this demand, many Thai camps are located right in the city. There are also lots of Thai camps throughout the country, and many of them are very good. Without question, though, most of the best camps are in Bangkok because this is where most fights are held and the biggest purses are offered.

Bangkok camps are often large and generally very busy. For this reason they may not be the best place for a beginner to train. As a general rule the newer the fighter is to the sport, the better it is for him to start training at a smaller camp; many of the smaller ones are in the countryside. More experienced fighters with a high level of skill will do well to train at one of the larger and more competitive camps near the center of the action in Bangkok.

In Villalobos' opinion, some of the really big camps in Bangkok are overly commercialized and overpriced. He believes that a reasonable fee for a week of training is currently between 1,000 and 2,000 baht, including lodging and food.

If a foreigner behaves respectfully, there is no reason to expect anything less than a local fighter does from the trainer. "If the trainer does not respond to you and show you attention and courtesy when you enter, you should consider it a warning sign and move on to the next camp," Villalobos advises.

The Muay Thai camp chosen to study in should have the equipment required for basic training, including: a Thai boxing ring, lots of Thai pads, headgear, uppercut wall pads, gloves, and at least seven or eight regular heavy bags (banana bags are not common in Thailand).

### Red Flags to Watch for When Selecting a Camp
- Trainer not correcting fighters
- Trainer not giving you any attention
- Pressure for money
- Lack of equipment equipment
- No champions
- Bad techniques
- Commercialization

### Things Not to Do While Staying in Camp
- Bring a woman into camp
- Touch anyone on the head
- Put your feet on a table
- Point with your feet
- Go out at night
- Miss curfew
- Enter a house with shoes on
- Be loud and rude

### Basic Rules for Getting Along at Camp
- Always return a bow
- Shower before eating
- Concentrate on training and nothing else
- Give 100-percent effort
- Bow when you enter the ring
- Bow when you exit the ring
- Bow to the trainer
- Be humble
- Show respect to everyone
- Open your heart
- Eat slowly
- Share your food
- Eat moderately
- Wash your Thai shorts frequently
- Stay clean

### Basic Thai Language for Training
Following are helpful words, numbers, and a basic vocabulary for Muay Thai. These are the words and expressions that a person needs when traveling to Thailand. Males should add the word *krup* at the end of every sentence. Females should add the word *ka* at the end of every sentence.

### General Expressions

| | |
|---|---|
| **Sawadeekrup** | Hello, good morning, good night |
| **Rawang** | Be careful |
| **Chai** | Yes |
| **Mai chai** | No |
| **Mai khao jae** | I don't understand |
| **Ao** | I want |
| **Mai ao** | I don't want |
| **Thong pae** | Go straight |
| **Kin khao** | Eat or eat rice |
| **Yut** | Stop |
| **Choke dee** | Good luck |
| **Khaw** | Right |
| **Sai** | Left |
| **Cha cha** | Go slow |
| **Kho thor krup** | I am sorry |
| **Pae lao** | He/she left |

| | | | |
|---|---|---|---|
| Dee mak | Very good | 31 | Saam sip et |
| Mai pe lae! | Doesn't matter! | 32 | Saam sip soom |
| Mai dee | Not good | 33 | Saam sip saam |
| Mak | Very | 40 | See sip |
| Ni | This | 41 | See sip et |
| Nick noi | Little bit | 42 | See sip soom |
| Choob | Like | 43 | See sip see |
| Mai choop | Don't like | 50 | Ha sip |
| Ti nae | Where | 51 | Ha sip et |
| Pom | I | 52 | Ha sip soom |
| Prattet alae? | Where are you from? | 53 | Ha sip saam |
| Koon | You (or Mr., Ms.) | 60 | Hook sip |
| Pet | Spice | 70 | Jet sip |
| Kaao | He/she | 80 | Peart sip |
| Naam yen | Cold water | 90 | Kao sip |
| A lai? | What? | 100 | Nung loy |
| Naam kang | Ice | 200 | Soom loy |
| Pom rak koon | I love you | 1,000 | Nung pan |
| Tao rae? | How much? | 2,000 | Soom pan |
| Yae | Big | 10,000 | Sip pan (or nung mun) |
| Lek | Small | | |
| Korp koon krup | Thank you | | |
| Lu | I know | | |
| Mai lu | I don't know | | |

*Thai Numbers*

| | | | |
|---|---|---|---|
| 1 | Nung | | |
| 2 | Soom | | |
| 3 | Saam | | |
| 4 | See | | |
| 5 | Haa | | |
| 6 | Hook | | |
| 7 | Jet | | |
| 8 | Peart | | |
| 9 | Kao | | |
| 10 | Sip | | |
| 11 | Sip et | | |
| 12 | Sip soom | | |
| 13 | Sip saam | | |
| 14 | Sip see | | |
| 15 | Sip haa | | |
| 16 | Sip hook | | |
| 17 | Sip jet | | |
| 18 | Sip peart | | |
| 19 | Sip kao | | |
| 20 | Yee sip | | |
| 21 | Yee sip et | | |
| 22 | Yee sip soom | | |
| 23 | Yee sip saam | | |
| 30 | Saam sip | | |

*Basic Muay Thai Training Vocabulary*

| | |
|---|---|
| Ajarn | Master |
| Chok | Fight |
| Dthey | Kick |
| Dtoi lom | Shadow boxing |
| Eo | Hips |
| Fai derng | Red corner |
| Fai namnerng (fa) | Blue corner |
| Farang | Foreigner |
| Garsawb | Punching bag |
| Gamagan | Referee |
| Gangken muay | Boxer shorts |
| Hua | Head |
| Kao (also ka) | Knee |
| Kao lov | Jumping knee |
| Kai muay | Boxing camp |
| Koon Thai | People of Thailand |
| Kru | Teacher |
| Kruang wrang | Amulet (arm band) |
| Muay sakon | Regular boxing (only hands) |
| Mat | Punch |
| Mongkon | Head band |
| Nak muay | Thai boxer |
| Nam nak | Weight |
| Nuam | Gloves |
| Ram muay | Ceremony dance (before fight) |
| Sit | Student |
| Sock | Elbow |
| Taa | Eye |

**FIGHTING STRATEGIES OF MUAY THAI**

| Taai | Die |
|---|---|
| **Teep** | Thrusting kick |
| **Tong** | Stomach |
| **Sanam muay** | Stadium of Thai boxing |
| **Wai kru** | Respect the teacher |
| **Wehtee** | Ring (or canvas) |

## MUAY THAI RULES AND REGULATIONS

The rules and regulations for Muay Thai matches in Thailand vary slightly from region to region. Most follow closely to the general overview that follows (Kraitus and Kraitus 1988, 233):

- Gloves are to weigh not more than 6 ounces and not less than 4 ounces.
- Fighters must weigh in between 9 and 12 hours before the start of the competition.
- Matches are conducted in five rounds of 3 minutes each.
- Each fighter may have up to two corner men.
- Each fight has one referee and two scoring judges.
- Each match has a timekeeper.
- Fighters must be over 17 and under 40 years of age.
- Fights are won by knockout, technical knockout, victory by points, victory by concession of one opponent, or victory by disqualification of one opponent.
- Fouls may result in a warning or in the forfeiture of the match at the discretion of the referee.
- Falls are defined as anytime that a boxer touches the floor with any part of his body other than feet, collapsing on the ropes, being knocked out of the ring, or standing defenselessly.
- Fighter shake hands before and after the match.

Thai boxers fight in weight classes. These classifications vary slightly between sanctioning organizations. Typical weight classes at Bangkok stadiums are as follows (Kraitus and Kraitus 1988):

| Class | Maximum Weight (in Pounds) |
|---|---|
| Bantamweight | 118 |
| Featherweight | 126 |
| Lightweight | 135 |
| Welterweight | 147 |
| Middleweight | 160 |
| Light heavyweight | 175 |
| Heavyweight | 175 and up |

The weight divisions in Thailand are different from those in the West because Thais tend to be smaller than their Western counterparts. In the United States, for example, the heavyweight class typically begins with fighters over 210 pounds.

## CONCLUSION

You can certainly become a brutal fighter by learning Thai technique and strategy, but violent power is not the primary goal of Muay Thai. The traditional Muay Thai practitioner seeks a balance of power and compassion, of ethics and spirituality, of confidence and humility.

"A man who has truly absorbed the art is always respectful and courteous, humble and self-disciplined. He is in constant control of his feelings, and can, at will, replace hot, volatile, and murky emotions with those that are cool and rational. He is as gentle as a lamb, as fierce as a lion" (Kraitus and Kraitus 1988, 3).

Muay Thai fighters in Thailand typically retire from professional competition by age 30 or sooner. Muay Thai practitioners, however, never quit. For many, Muay Thai is a lifelong experience. Young and old practice Muay Thai for many reasons. Whether an individual fights in the professional Muay Thai circuit or practices Muay Thai for self-defense and self-knowledge does not matter so much as the fact that he participates. Muay Thai boxing is far more than a competitive sport; it is a martial art in the fullest sense of the term.

Pedro Solana Villalobos believes in the value of a person's transforming himself into the best person that he can possibly be. He sees the martial arts as a tool for discovery worthy of one's full focus. Villalobos is mindful that winning against an opponent is not nearly as important as learning about self and growing physically, mentally, and spiritually in the process. Villalobos sees Muay Thai training as a rich, cultural experience through which one travels for the purpose of developing oneself, serving others, and serving the world.

# APPENDIX VILLALOBOS' PROFESSIONAL FIGHT TEAM

### PEDRO SOLANA VILLALOBOS

Age: 29
Height: 5' feet 9 inches
Weight: 160 pounds
Country: Spain
Fights: 15 (Wins, 12; Losses, 3; Draws, 0)

*Championships:*
- 1994 Light Middleweight Kickboxing Amateur Champion of Spain (WAKO Association)
- U.S. 1998 ISKA Middleweight Muay Thai Champion in the Professional Division
- 1998 Submission Open in Griffin, Georgia, Champion
- 1998 SFO Lightweight Champion
- 1999 Battle of Koh Samui (Thailand) Champion

Contact Villalobos at <thailandartsinstitute@hotmail.com>.

### RICHARD "TCHALLA" TRAMMELL

Age: 34
Height: 5 feet 10 inches
Weight: 155 pounds
Country: United States
Fights: 23 (Wins, 22; Losses, 1; Draws, 0)

*Championships:*
- 1988 ISKA Light Middleweight U.S. Champion
- 2000 Shidokan Lightweight U.S. Champion
- 2000 North American Shidokan Champion
- 2001 Shikon Muay Thai Champion

## LANE "LIGHTNING" COLLYER

Age: 32
Height: 6 feet 2 inches
Weight: 220 pounds
Country: United States

**Amateur Career:**
Fights: 28 (Wins, 24; Losses, 4; KOs, 16)

*Championships:*
- 1993–1994 ISKA Georgia Cruiserweight Champion
- 1993–1998 ISKA Georgia Heavyweight Champion
- 1994–1988 ISKA Region Cruiserweight Champion
- 1995–1998 WKA S.E. Region Superheavyweight Champion
- 1988–1998 I.S.K.A. Intercontinental Cruiserweight Champion
- 1988–1998 ISKA World Heavyweight Champion

**Professional Career:**
Fights: 2 (Wins, 2; Losses, 0; KOs, 1)

*Championships:*
- 1999–2000 ISKA Georgia Heavyweight State Champion
- 2000 IFF U.S. Heavyweight Muay Thai Champion

# BIBLIOGRAPHY

Clausewitz, C. *On War*. Translated by Colonel J.J. Graham. London: N. Trübner, 1873.

De Cesaris, M. *Boxeo Thailandes Muay Thai*. Tutor. Madrid: 2000.

Dempsey, J. *Championship Fighting, Explosive Punching and Aggressive Defense*. Downey, Calif.: Centerline Press, 1950.

Fairtex, <http://www.fairtexbkk.com/>.

Heiman, S.E.; D. Sanchez; and T. Tuleja. *The New Strategic Selling*. New York: Warner Books, 1985.

Hellenic Amateur Muay Thai Federation. <http://www.hfmtk.gr/>.

International Amateur Muay Thai Federation (IAMTF). <http://www.iamtf.org/>.

International Federation of Muay Thai Amateur (IFMA). <http://www.wmcifma.com/>.

Kraitus, Panya and Pitisuk Kraitus. *Muay Thai, The Most Distinguished Art of Fighting*. Bangkok: Mr. Panya Kraitus, 1988.

Lee, B. *Tao of Jeet Kune Do*. Burbank, Calif.: Ohara Publications, Inc., 1975.

McNeilly, M. *Sun Tzu and the Art of Business, Six Strategic Principles for Managers*. New York and Oxford: Oxford University Press, 1988.

*Muay Thai News*. <http://www.angelfire.com/ca/muaythaiusa/News.html>.

Muaythai online. <http://www.muaythaionline.net./>.

Muaythai.com. <http://muaythai.com/>.

Rebac, Z. *Thai Boxing Dynamite, the Explosive art of Muay Thai*. Boulder, Colo.: Paladin Press, 1987.

Turner, K., and M. Van Schuyver. *Secrets of Championship Karate*. Chicago: Contemporary Books, 1991.

UK Muay Thai Federation. <http://www.muaythai.co.uk/>.

United States Muay Thai Association. <http://www.usmta.com/>.

Von Ghyczy, T.; B. Von Oetinger; and C. Bassfort. *Clausewitz on Strategy*. New York: John Wiley & Sons, Inc., 2001.

Warehouse Martial Arts. <http://www.warehousemartialarts.com/>.

World Muay Thai Organization. <http://www.wmto.org/>.

World Muaythai Council (WMC). <http://www.wmtc.nu/>.

# GLOSSARY

**aerobic exercises**—Exercises that keep one doing the same thing for a long time at the same pace, such as even running or cycling or hitting a bag at the same pace.

**aggressive fighter**—Fighter type that uses raw power to win. One of the four types of fighter.

**anaerobic exercises**—Exercises that push the heart rate up very high, let it fall back down, and then push it up again.

**banana bag**—A very tall heavy bag.

**belly pad**—Special pad that Thai trainers strap around their midsection when working full-contact techniques with their fighters.

**Brazilian jiu-jitsu**—Brazil's version of jujutsu that relies heavily on ground grappling and submission.

**circle knee**—Circular Muay Thai knee strikes usually done in the clinch.

**circle of death**—Intense Muay Thai heavy-bag training routines.

**clinch**—When two fighters hold on to each other and continue to fight. Clinch is the fourth range for Muay Thai fighting. *Plam* means clinch in Thai.

**counter fighter**—Strategically defensive fighters who use counterattacks to win. One of the four types of fighter.

**elusive fighter**—A fast fighter who uses speed and timing to win. One of the four types of fighter.

**evading**—Moving out of the way of an incoming attack

**flying elbow**—An elbow delivered by leaping above the opponent and driving the power downward.

**flying knee**—Muay Thai knee attack done by leaping at the opponent.

**focus mitts**—Hand-held punching mitts used to catch punches.

**foot jab**—Thai boxing's version of the front kick.

**four ranges of Muay Thai**—Kicking, punching, knee and elbow, and clinching.

**four types of fighter**—Aggressive, elusive, counter, and tricky.

**gravitation**—Gravitational pull of the Earth that makes all Muay Thai techniques possible. One of the seven powers of Muay Thai.

**guard**—The protective position in which the hands are held.

**invisible kick**—A close-range Muay Thai round kick that rises at such an angle that it is very difficult for an opponent to see coming.

**judo**—Japanese throwing art.

**jujutsu (jiu-jitsu in Brazilian form)**—Japanese grappling and submission art.

**karate**—Japanese martial art.

**keun kru** (also called yok kru)—This is a ritual of acceptance to training, and it is performed before an image of Buddha, typically on a Thursday. This ritual happens after an apprenticeship period and at a time when the instructor is ready to formally accept the student and the student accepts the instructor and agrees to follow the rules. The student promises loyalty to the teacher during this ritual.

**kickboxing**—Usually refers to Western-style fighting with gloved hands in which kicks and punches to limited targets are legal.

**kicking range**—First of four ranges of Muay Thai fighting.

**knee-and-elbow range**—Third of four ranges of Muay Thai fighting.

**krabi-krabong**—Ancient Thai martial art featuring weapons and empty-hand fighting techniques. Krabi-krabong is still taught today.

**kronb kru**—The ceremony that happens upon the completion of a fighter's training and at a point at which the fighter is able to compete at a high-level and also competent to instruct others in the art.

**kru**—Thai for instructor of Muay Thai (sometimes spelled *khru*).

**L-bag**—Special Muay Thai training bag used to practice uppercuts.

**mixed martial arts**—Martial arts schools that mix a variety of arts to formulate a complete curriculum. Muay Thai or at lease some Muay Thai techniques are often included, as are throwing and ground fighting skills.

**momentum**—The quantity of motion of a moving object equal to the product of its mass and its velocity.

**mongkon**—Ceremonial headband worn by fighters before a match.

**Muay Thai**—Also known as Muay Thai boxing or simply Thai boxing. A martial art and ring sport from Thailand

**Muay Thai Boran**—Old Muay Thai. Muay Thai Boran is a generic term for any version of Muay Thai that existed before the government of Thailand regulated the sport in the early part of the 20th century. Muay Thai Boran is the forerunner of modern Muay Thai. A living version of Muay Thai Boran is part of the krabi-krabong martial art system still practiced today.

**Muay Thai massage**—Special pre- and postfight massages given to fighters to loosen muscles, relax the body, and accelerate the recovery process.

**parrying**—Deflecting an incoming attack.

**plam lam**—Neck wrestling or clinch fighting. Clinching is the fourth range in Muay Thai fighting.

**punching range**—Second of four ranges of Muay Thai fighting.

**ram muay**—Literally, "boxing dance." Part of the ritual dance performed before each fight. The ram muay signifies respect for the spirits of Muay Thai.

**ring**—The ring in which Muay Thai matches are fought.

**rotation**—Turning of the hip when delivering a strike. One of the seven powers of Muay Thai.

**rounds**—Short increments of time in which Thai boxers train and fight. Match rounds are typically 5 minutes long. Training rounds vary in length. Rounds are always followed by a short rest period.

**sarama**—The music played during Muay Thai bouts.

**seven powers of Muay Thai**—Transition, velocity, rotation, snap, torque, triangulation, and gravitation.

**shielding**—Allowing the opponent's punch, elbow, knee, or kick to land upon one's elbow, knee, or other hardened body part as a way of defending oneself.

**snap**—Quick forward motion of the shoulder done when punching or throwing an elbow in Muay Thai. Also refers to the sharp turning of the foot performed in Muay Thai round kicking. One of the seven powers of Muay Thai.

**spinning elbow**—An elbow delivered by spinning around.

**strategy**—What one does to prepare for a fight.

**switch**—Any time a Muay Thai fighter changes the lead side of the body.

**ta pong (or glong kag)**—Two-faced drum played during Muay Thai fights.

**tactic**—The application of strategy and technique in a combat situation.

**tae kwon so**—Korean martial art.

**technique**—An offensive or defensive skill used in fighting.

**Thai boxing**—Also known as Muay Thai. A martial art and ring sport from Thailand.

**Thailand Arts Institute**—Kru Pedro Villalobos' Muay Thai boxing and krabi-krabong school in Atlanta, Georgia.

**Thai camps**—Schools located in Thailand where fighters live and learn Muay Thai.

**Thai pads**—Special striking pads that fit on the forearms.

**torque**—Spinning of the hand during a punch just before impact. One of the seven powers of Muay Thai.

**transition**—Energy gained from motion relative to the opponent. One of the seven powers of Muay Thai.

**triangulation**—Dropping of the hand, elbow, or foot upon impact with the target that drives the energy of the strike downward. One of the seven powers of Muay Thai.

**tricky fighter**—Fighter who uses deception to win. One of the four types of fighter.

**universal fighter**—The rare individual who can fight at will in the style of all of the four types of Muay Thai fighter: aggressive, counter, elusive, and tricky.

**velocity**—Speed of the body and of the body weapon as it approaches the target. One of the seven powers of Muay Thai.

**Villalobos**—City of wolves.

**wai kru**—Ritual performed by each fighter before every competition. It is done to show respect to the fighter's teacher and teacher's teacher. It also expresses respect for the king, the person overseeing the matches, and to God. The wai kru also serves to focus the fighter's concentration and loosen the muscles before fighting.

**we wai kru**—The annual ceremony dedicated to teachers in which students renew their promise of loyalty and respect.

**wing chun**—Chinese martial art that features control of the centerline.

# ABOUT THE AUTHOR

Mark Van Schuyver (van-sky-ver) has practiced martial arts for many years. Currently he is studying Brazilian jiu-jitsu under Professor Jacare' Cavalcanti at Professor Jacare's Alliance Brazilian Jiu-Jitsu school in Atlanta, Georgia.

Van Schuyver is the author of *Secrets of Championship Karate* (with coauthor Karyn Turner), as well as more than 100 nonfiction articles in such national magazines as *Black Belt, Inside Kung-Fu, Karate/Kung-Fu Illustrated, Karate Illustrated, Fighter, MA Training*, and *Tae Kwon Do Times*. He can be reached by email at <VanSchuyver@mindspring.com>.

(For a lengthy biography of Kru Pedro Solana Villalobos, see the Preface, pages xiv–xvii, and the Appendix, pages 129–130.)

# If you liked this book, you will also want to read these:

## MUAY THAI KICKBOXING
### The Ultimate Guide to Conditioning, Training, and Fighting
#### by Chad Boykin
Whether you long to test yourself in the ring or simply get in the best shape of your life, this book shows you how. Let a ring veteran train you in the workouts that provide power and speed, the brutal strikes, kicks and clenches that form your offensive arsenal and the blocks and evasions that will baffle your opponent. 8 1/2 x 11, softcover, 430 photos, illus., 216 pp.

**#MTK**

## THAI BOXING
### Produced by Zoran Rebac
Get a guided tour of the savage world of Thai boxing as you've never seen it before, including its history, traditions, techniques and training, all shot on location in the gyms and boxing rings of Thailand. Includes hard-hitting fight highlights of some of Thailand's toughest boxers shot in Lumpinee Stadium in Bangkok. Color, approx. 50 min.

**#THAIV**

## TRADITIONAL BURMESE BOXING
### Ancient and Modern Methods
### from Burma's Training Camps
#### by Zoran Rebac
Through rare photographs and firsthand reports, enter a world few Westerners have ever seen. Learn traditional Burmese boxing techniques from the basic stances, kicks and strikes through advanced "experts only" moves, and be introduced to the grueling training exercises practiced in ancient times and the modern methods used by fighters today. 8 1/2 x 11, softcover, photos, 128 pp.

**#TBB**

## BURMESE BOXING
### The Last Gladiators of Asia
### Produced by Zoran Rebac
Burmese boxing includes all the bone-breaking punches, elbows, knees and kicks that characterize Thai boxing; however, it also incorporates devastating head butts, spinning strikes and even dramatic vaulting attacks. This amazing video features a look at its history, rare footage of boxing demonstrations by Burmese masters, instruction in its basic fighting techniques and counters, and the rules of modern Burmese boxing. *For academic study only.* Color, approx. 50 min.

**#BBV**

## PANANANDATA
### History and Techniques of the Daga, Yantok, Balisong, and Other
### Weapons of the Philippines
#### by Amante Marinas Sr.
Not since Dan Inosanto's classic *The Filipino Martial Arts* has one book encompassed so many different aspects of the arts of the Philippines. Marinas teaches the fighting techniques of such weapons as the *dikin* (ring), *hawakan* (tonfa), *latiko* (whip), blowgun, *tabak toyok* (nunchaku) and more. 8 1/2 x 11, softcover, photos, 160 pp.

**#PAN**

## FILIPINO KUNTAO
### The Art of Jing Shen Jie Fang "Free Spirit" Fighting
#### with Prof. Rick Hernandez
Filipino kuntao is a savage fighting art that combines the crippling low-line kicks of Filipino *sikaran* with the rapid-fire strikes of the Chinese arts In this two-tape set, kuntao master Rick Hernandez presents a comprehensive training program that reveals the secrets of this deadly art. *For academic study only.* Color, approx. 150 min. total.

**#FKV**

## INDONESIAN FIGHTING FUNDAMENTALS
### The Brutal Arts of the Archipelago
#### by Bob Orlando
The fighting arts of Indonesia, a mix of pentjak silat and Chinese kuntao, were never meant for sport: they are brutal, unrelenting and designed to take the enemy out and punish him every step of the way. This unprecedented book by a long-time student of Dutch-Indonesian Master Willem de Thouars shows you why. 8 1/2 x 11, softcover, over 350 photos, illus., 200 pp.

**#IFF**

## THAI BOXING DYNAMITE
### The Explosive Art of Muay Thai
#### by Zoran Rebac
You're in the ring when three flashing kicks from the Muay Thai boxer knock you to the canvas. Muay Thai, the hottest style of kickboxing to hit the sports world, integrates the use of legs and fists in one clean, fluid, yet savage style. Get the facts on how to master *Thai Boxing Dynamite.* 8 1/2 x 11, softcover, photos, 120 pp.

**#TB**